He Knew I Would Tell

Short Stories of God Moments in the Lives of Ordinary People

By Cheryl Mochau

with additional stories by:

Marlina Easton
Cheryl Brown Folz
Robin Lannert
Vicki Brasel
Phil Young
Christa Shore
Peggy Shorter
Gary Shorter
Cindy McClanahan

He Knew I Would Tell

Short Stories of God Moments in the Lives of Ordinary People

Cheryl Mochau

authorHOUSE®

AuthorHouse™
1663 Liberty Drive
Bloomington, IN 47403
www.authorhouse.com
Phone: 1-800-839-8640

Cover Photograph © 2010 Edwards Images Photography.

First published by AuthorHouse   11/2/2010

ISBN: 978-1-4259-6548-8 (sc)

Printed in the United States of America

This book is printed on acid-free paper.

Dedication

To God, the Creator of the heavens and earth.

To His Holy Spirit, the very essence of God Himself.

To Jesus, the Son of God, Savior to all who call on Him.

No greater love exists!

Table of Contents

Acknowledgments

About two years ago, God put it on my heart to write this book, *He Knew I Would Tell*. The material presented itself easily enough, but it took a year and a half for me to get focused enough to start. Time management was the problem.

The art of balancing home life and full time work outside the home, while trying to be a good wife and sister in the faith, has always been a struggle for me. My husband, Geoff, has heard my time crunch complaints more than anyone. His frequent response? "God gave you just as much time as He gave everyone else. Success comes with managing it well."

Going to God in prayer, I asked Him to help me make the best use of the time available. Starting the next morning, and most mornings for the following five-and-a-half months, I awoke at four o'clock and started writing until about seven, when it was time to get ready for work. You hold in your hands what tumbled out onto paper during that time.

> Jesus was teaching and was asked, *"What must we do to do the works God requires?" Jesus answered, "The work of God is this: to believe in the One He has sent."* JOHN 6:28

So you don't get the wrong idea and think I wrote this all by myself, please realize that my husband, Geoff, as well as my brother and several of my friends came alongside me to help. They all offered their own special stories and talents and I am grateful and indebted to each of them!

Marlina Easton taught me how to walk through the narrow gate straight into Jesus' arms almost two decades ago. With boldness and urgency she has done the same for many others, before and since.

Phil Young shared how the prayers of a community brought him before God for healing.

Cheryl Brown Folz shared how God surprised her twice over.

Gary and Peggy Shorter have both been touched by God and enjoy telling the details. They believe God wants the stories told.

Robin Lannert traveled halfway around the world to find and feed the love in her heart. At the time of this writing she has just returned from her third trip overseas to see "her kids".

Christa Shore has the heart of a prayer warrior. Her relationship with God is evident and she blesses everyone she comes in contact with.

Vicki Brasel grew her faith in God after losing someone she loves. Her prayer is to finish her earthly journey with those God puts in her heart.

Cindy "Moe" McClanahan sprinkles the love of Jesus into everything she cooks and gets perfect results, every time.

Special thanks to my Tuesday morning Bible study group, "The Prayer Warrior Chicks", for their prayers and support.

Annette McDonald helped to edit these stories so the words

would flow easily and the messages would be clear. I am especially grateful to Annette, and her red pen, for the time and expertise she used to help share these stories.

Geoff, my beloved husband, will probably be the happiest of anyone when this book finally goes to press. Life in our household has been far from normal lately. Geoff patiently edited and formatted each story into a single unified package. I am thankful for his help and would not have finished this book without him.

My sincere thanks go to the many others who told me stories of their rich God moments so I could write them down.

Whoever tries to keep his life will lose it, and whoever loses his life will preserve it. LUKE 17:33

Living Water

No human has ever learned how to make water. Yet water has always existed and is crucial for all living things to exist.

> *"In the beginning God created the heavens and the earth. Now the earth was formless and empty, darkness was over the surface of the deep, and the Spirit of God was hovering over the waters."* GENESIS 1:1

Over thirty years ago, when I lived in northwest Connecticut, I enjoyed bicycling in the rural countryside. There was a ravine at the end of one long stretch of highway that was a destination stop. Even in the heat of summer, a steady stream of water tumbled off the nearby mountain, forming perfect pools of cold water to cool off in. Thick, lush moss grew at the edges of the pools and covered the surrounding rocks, making them look and feel like velvet pillows.

My mother was in the last stages of cancer when I took her there. We drove her car and parked it in the autumn sun, just past the bridge. Across the highway the water crashed and roared its way out from under the bridge. I wanted to save that dynamic scene for last, so we turned north and entered a woodsy area by way of a well-worn horse trail.

Slowly, we made our way to the water's edge. The water tinkled and gurgled its way over the rocks, swirled lazily around in two large pools, and then continued on toward the cascading waterfall on the other side of the bridge.

For the teenager in me, it was a beautiful place to refresh myself in the middle of a long bike ride. For my mom, it became her sanctuary.

Slowly, she lowered her aching body onto a moss-covered rock and caught her breath. In time, she leaned over and dipped her hand into the water. Cupping her hand and drawing the water to her lips she said, "This is holy water. I can feel The Lord in it." She scooped up the water in her hands and splashed it on her face, ran it through her hair, and on her arms, not caring that her blouse was getting wet. She slipped off her shoes and touched her feet to the water, but pulled back quickly from the cold of it. Laughing and talking with energy she had not had for months, she delighted in the presence of The Lord.

> John the Baptist said, *"After me will come One more powerful than I, the thongs of whose sandals I am not worthy to stoop down and untie. I baptize you with water, but He will baptize you with the Holy Spirit."* MARK 1:7

My mom and I talked that day by the pool about all the things we wanted to share. We were both blessed by the cleansing water.

Before getting back into the car, we walked across the highway to get a top view of the cascading waterfall. The late afternoon sun shone through the trees, casting dappled light on the rushing, roaring falls that shot out from the bridge beneath our feet.

The falls were beautiful, even from the top angle. Leaning over the rail, I thanked God for the constant flow of Holy Water that seemed to pour fresh life into my mom. It was comforting knowing that long after she was gone, the water would continue to flow.

> Jesus said, *"If you knew the gift of God and Who it is that asks you for a drink, you would have asked Him and He would have given you living water."* JOHN 4:10

Jesus referred to Himself as Living Water. No one can make their own water, and no one can get to Father God without going through Jesus. So water turns out to be a perfect metaphor for our beloved Jesus, The Christ. Humans need Christ (cleansing and nourishing) to connect to God (life and love), who in turn gives them the gift of The Holy Spirit (knowledge and power). It's a perfect three-part package. Whoever coined the phrase "three's a crowd" wasn't thinking of this Masterful Trinity!

> Jesus said to the Samaritan woman, *"Everyone who drinks this water will be thirsty again, but whoever drinks the water I give him will never thirst. Indeed, the water I give him will become in him a spring of water welling up to eternal life."* JOHN 4:13

Leaning over the rail, I thanked God for the constant flow of Holy Water that seemed to pour fresh life into my mom. It was comforting knowing that long after she was gone, the water would continue to flow.

God's Awesome Hand

God's awesome power is so frequently used for the benefit of His loved ones that we sometimes take it for granted and miss the opportunity to give Him thanks and praise for it. The next story is my first real recollection of God's Hand ensuring my safety.

I grew up on a large farm with my parents, five older brothers and a younger sister. Everyone had chores to do, and all the kids grew up fast and strong.

When I was four years old, my six-year-old brother Rick and I were hitching a ride on the back of a tractor while our nine-year-old brother, Fred, drove. We had heard it before, but Fred specifically told both of us not to step on the large metal pin that connected the trailer to the tractor, because the motion of the pin would throw us off. Being four years old and forgetful, I stepped on it momentarily, to shift my weight, and was instantly thrust under the rolling trailer. Rick pounded on Fred's back to alert him, and Fred stopped the tractor within a hair's breadth of my tiny ribs getting crushed under the back wheels of the trailer.

Both brothers yelled at me incessantly, asking why I didn't crawl out as soon as I hit the ground. I really didn't know why

I couldn't crawl all the way out. I told them that those few seconds went by in slow motion, just like in a movie. I knew I had slipped, and felt the sharpness of dried hay stubble on my arms and legs. When I hit the ground, instinct must have kicked in, because half of my body was out from under the trailer when they stopped. The back wheel of the trailer was lined up to crush my midsection.

When the shouting was over, the boys cuddled me in consolation and took me home. Each of us had been shaken to the core by the incident and would have to tell our mother and the rest of the family the details.

> *Stern discipline awaits him who leaves the path; he who hates correction will die.* PROVERBS 15:10

I have always believed that God spared me, as much for myself as for them. That kind of tragedy would have killed me, but would have had devastating repercussions for the whole family for the rest of their lives. Life on a farm can be hard, but it would be even worse after a tragedy like that one. I believe that a power greater than ourselves saved us all that day.

> *The Lord watches over you — the Lord is your shade at your right hand; the sun will not harm you by day, nor the moon by night. The Lord will keep you from all harm — He will watch over your life; The Lord will watch over your coming and going both now and forevermore.* PSALM 121:5

I have always believed that God spared me, as much for myself, as for them. That kind of tragedy would have killed me, but would have had devastating repercussions for the whole family for the rest of their lives.

Barstool Angels

Trouble seems to brew in bars, and I think that's why angels frequent them.

Ivan Record must have had one of those angels that hung out in bars. Ivan liked to drink whiskey, smoke fat cigars, chew tobacco and cuss. Wow, could that man cuss! He never married, nor had children of his own. None that he spoke of, anyway.

My father also frequented bars, and one night he brought Ivan home because he didn't have a place to stay. This gesture of kindness and generosity might create some confusion about who the real angel was. I'm getting ahead of myself here.

My mother was pregnant with me when Ivan first came to live with us. My parents had just moved my five brothers to a larger house out in the country. There would be a few more moves in the next five years until we finally rented a huge farm in New York State. My father had gotten a "deal" on the rent. His boys were going to run the farm and he would go back to live and work in the city to make ends meet. He would come to the farm on weekends. Most weekends. Okay, maybe just some weekends.

Ivan Record was with us the whole time. He helped my brothers rebuild the barn and learn how to be dairy farmers. In his day, Ivan had been a finish carpenter. He also knew how to pour concrete and was a pretty good landscaper. As it turned out, for a man's man, Ivan was quite a catch! He enjoyed his work, and helped my brothers and my father (when he was around) build the dilapidated farm into a reasonably profitable operation.

If only Ivan hadn't smoked fat cigars, spat chewing tobacco juice around, drank whiskey and cussed. It was those things that made my mother get mad at him regularly.

The years went by — fifteen to be exact. Ivan put his mark all over that rented farm. My parents finally divorced. They were waiting for the kids to grow up, but too many "moments of weakness", as my mother put it, brought more kids into the picture. My mother had been diagnosed with breast cancer, and that must have been the last straw, because finally, they just called it quits.

Not long after, my mother met a man at a Christmas party where she worked. He was the father of one of her co-workers. They hit it off and were married less than a year later. My sister and I moved into his house with our mom and lived there for several years. He helped her through her cancer treatments, and soon after, she helped him through his. They were good for each other.

Meanwhile, back at the farm, my brothers worked for a few more years. Ivan stayed with them, but was soon diagnosed with leukemia. When he could no longer take care of himself, he turned himself over to become a ward of the state and moved out. As Ivan's angel had done before, he found him a place to call home, and it was only a few miles away. This time it was with a retired doctor and his wife.

The doctor oversaw Ivan's cancer treatments. His wife saw to his spiritual side.

There was only our family and the doctor and his wife at Ivan's funeral. My mother had ordered a casket drape made of white carnations with seven red roses, one for each of us kids, who Ivan had helped bring up.

After the short funeral service, we talked with the doctor and his wife. She told us that Ivan had accepted Jesus as his personal Savior before he died. She and my mother talked for quite a bit, while the rest of us waited nearby.

On the ride home after the funeral, my mother tried to explain what the doctor's wife had said about Ivan and Jesus. We knew Ivan as a rough old guy who always smelled of bourbon and tobacco. And we knew he could cuss, so how did he and Jesus ever see eye to eye?

> Jesus said, *"All that belongs to the Father is mine. That is why I said the Spirit will take from what is mine and make it known to you."* JOHN 16:15

Ivan's death sparked an interest in Jesus for my mother. She started taking my sister and me to church, and talking about Him regularly. When the evangelist Billy Graham ran a special on television, my mother would be sure to watch it. My mother was growing her faith and she wanted us to join her.

One night a Billy Graham special was scheduled to come on television, and my mother requested that my sister, our stepfather and I all sit and watch it with her. When Billy asked those who believed in Jesus to come to the front of the auditorium, my mother asked us to accept Jesus right there in our living room. And we all did.

From within our freshly cleansed souls from Jesus, we prayed for the rest of our family who had not yet accepted Him as their personal Savior. We wanted all of them to come with us into the Kingdom of God.

Cheryl Mochau

God sends his angels wherever lives need to change. The angel who warmed the barstool next to Ivan and my father had his work cut out for him. As God would have it, it was a fruitful harvest. By human standards it was a long time coming, and almost didn't happen. By God's standard it was business as usual.

> Jesus said, "... Rejoice with me; I have found my lost sheep. I tell you that in the same way there will be more rejoicing in heaven over one sinner who repents than over ninety-nine righteous persons who do not need to repent." LUKE 15:6

We knew Ivan as a rough old guy who always smelled of bourbon and tobacco. And we knew he could cuss, so how did he and Jesus ever see eye to eye?

Keeping Secrets

Jesus knew the secrets of heaven and earth. He was best friends with mortals during His time in the flesh, and it's safe to bet that Jesus knew their limits when it came to keeping secrets.

Jesus must have given it a great deal of thought before He invited Peter, James and James' brother, John, to climb with Him alone up a nearby mountain. There is controversy among biblical scholars whether it was Mount Hermon or Mount Tabor, but that aside, the men *did* climb a mountain and they *did* have an incredible mountain-top experience when they got there!

Witnessing the transfiguration of Jesus must have been the most surreal moment the three former fishermen could ever imagine happening — up to that moment, anyway. First, Matthew 17:1 reveals, Jesus' "*… face shown like the sun, and His clothes became as white as the light. Just then there appeared before them Moses and Elijah, talking with Jesus.*" I don't know about you, but that tops anything I have ever seen in my life. And I would have a hard time keeping it a secret. But if Jesus said to me, as he did to the disciples in Matthew 17:9, "*Don't tell anyone what you have seen, until the Son of Man has been raised from the dead.*" then I want to believe that I would be strong enough to keep it to myself. If I understood that letting the details out would bring about Jesus' death sooner, then I hope I would see the importance of keeping the secret quiet for as long as necessary. And to be sure the others did, too.

It had only been six days before they climbed the mountain, when Peter took Jesus aside and rebuked Him for talking about His upcoming death and resurrection. That's how close these men were with the Son of God. So close that they spoke freely, to the point of telling Him to stop talking about Him being killed and rising on the third day. It was out of love that Peter rebuked Jesus.

Imagine Peter's reaction when Jesus returned fire with fire in Matthew 16:23: *Jesus turned and said to Peter, "Get behind me, Satan! You are a stumbling block to me; and you do not have in mind the things of God, but the things of men."*

It's likely that six days later as they took the mountain trip, Peter still stung from those horrible words spoken by his beloved friend Jesus. Peter probably wanted to do anything possible to be right with Jesus. That may be why he suggested that he, James, and John build shelters for Jesus, Moses, and Elijah. After all, Peter was only human.

Before Peter could even finish offering to build them shelters, Matthew 17:5 tells us that God Himself appeared and spoke: ... *A bright cloud enveloped them, and a voice from the cloud said, "This is my Son, whom I love; with Him I am well pleased. Listen to Him!"* The disciples dropped to the ground hiding their faces. *But Jesus came and touched them. "Get up," He said. "Don't be afraid." When they looked up, they saw no one except Jesus.*

The long walk down the mountain must have been an interesting one. Jesus told the disciples not to tell anyone what had happened on the mountain until after He had been raised from the dead. In Matthew 17:10 the disciples asked Jesus, *"Why then do the teachers of the law say that Elijah must come first?" Jesus replied, "To be sure, Elijah comes and will restore all things. But I tell you, Elijah has already come, and they did not recognize him, but have done to him everything they wished. In the same way the Son of Man is going to suffer at their hands." Then the disciples understood that He was talking to them about John the Baptist.*

From what the three men had just witnessed, they knew that Elijah, Moses and Jesus were actively talking together. God Himself came in the form of a bright cloud and spoke, so the three men would not miss the point, telling them that Jesus was His Son, that He loved Him and was pleased with Him. God finished by telling the men to listen to Jesus!

The three men came to understand that Jesus' death was as critical as His life. They were not to interfere, but to let God's plan fall into place for the benefit of His future glory. To tell what they had seen prematurely would have raised red flags all around Jesus and the work of The Lord would be compromised. Peter, James and his brother, John, all had to carry the weight of the secret, of Jesus' transformation, until after Jesus was raised from the dead. Little did they realize how short a time that would actually be. That Jesus chose those three men to witness His transfiguration and the meeting with Moses and Elijah shows that He believed in them more than they could ever believe in themselves.

How good are you at keeping secrets? Do secrets burn on your tongue until you break down and release them to someone else? Even though you may have sworn them to secrecy, does the next person who hears it respect the secret any more than you did?

> Jesus explains, *"But the things that come out of the mouth come from the heart, and these make a man 'unclean'."*
> MATTHEW 15:18

On Tuesday mornings several of my friends and I meet at church from 8:30 to 10:00 to share how God is alive in our lives. We study scripture and the works of current inspirational writers, and then share how it fits into our lives. Secrets are shared in that room. We all know that once shared, they are never to be repeated. There is safety in knowing that each of us has shared secrets, therefore we would not want to breach the trust of any of the other women.

> Jesus teaches, *"So in everything, do to others what you would have them do to you, for this sums up the Law and the Prophets."* MATTHEW 7:12

Prayer is very helpful when it comes to keeping secrets. The deliberate act of asking the Holy Spirit for help in keeping a secret safe is probably one of the easier tasks people ask of Him. If you must share the secrets you have been trusted with, share them with The Holy Spirit alone. He will have already heard all about it anyway, so your secret will be safe with Him.

> Because He Himself suffered when He was tempted, He is able to help those who are being tempted. HEBREWS 2:18

The three men came to understand that Jesus' death was as critical as His life.

God's Crack of Dawn

When you look at the sins of your past, do they leave you feeling absolutely positive that you have destroyed any chance of ever being acceptable to God? Does the thought of Judgement Day have you warming up to the idea of hell fires burning around you for eternity? Well, forget all that! Jesus wants you to learn who He is and how to follow Him to spend eternity with God.

Jesus wants you to believe in Him as the Son of God, and in His ability and desire to forgive all mankind of sins. Jesus has said that forgiven souls smell fresh and sweet to God. All forgiveness starts with accepting Jesus.

God sent Jesus to earth to teach those who would listen that God loves all people. Though He has stirred up controversy by showing up unannounced in a burning bush, and feeding the wandering Jews nothing but manna for years on end, God does everything out of love for His creations.

Love, as we have come to find out from those who knew Him, is also the total make up of Jesus. Yes, *is*, as in present tense, because although Jesus walked the face of the earth two thousand years ago, His spirit was alive before that, in the beginning of time, is still alive today, and will be forever.

The Apostle John was in Ephesus during the years of 90-96 A.D. when he wrote about the life and times of Jesus. He opened his book explaining that Jesus, whom he called *the Word*, is the Son of God. He wrote that Jesus has always been with God, even before the earth was formed.

> *In the beginning was the Word, and the Word was with God, and the Word was God. He was with God in the beginning.* JOHN 1:1

Genesis 1:1-2 tells us *In the beginning God created the heavens and the earth. Now the earth was formless and empty, darkness was over the surface of the deep, and the Spirit of God was hovering over the waters.*

Right there we are introduced to God and shown that He has a spirit. In the next sentence we are shown the creation of day and night. Jesus is frequently referred to as *the Light* numerous times in the pages ahead. If it's true that Jesus has always been with God, then it isn't unusual that God named the light of day after His Son, *Light*.

> *And God said, "Let there be light", and there was light. God saw that the light was good, and He separated the light from the darkness.* GENESIS 1:3

Then in Genesis 1:26 God goes on to say *"... Let us make man in our image, in our likeness, and let them rule over the fish of the sea and birds of the air, over the livestock, over all the earth, and over all the creatures that move along the ground."*

We can assume that He wasn't just talking to Himself, but to the Holy Spirit that hovered in Him over the waters of the deep, and with *the Light*, whom we now know as Jesus, who would one day become the light of men and women throughout the universe.

Through Him all things were made; without Him nothing was made that had been made. JOHN 1:3

This is the Apostle John's way of telling us that Jesus was *with* God during the formation of the earth.

The greatest scientists that ever lived couldn't possibly fathom the intensity of those brainstorming sessions! Imagine the insight required to design the core of the earth, its internal fires and springs of water that would form the external volcanoes, mountains, deserts, streams and rivers. The design had to run like clockwork, to regenerate life of all kinds, until the end of time. Imagine developing various trees, shrubs, and plants that would thrive in the assorted climates of the constantly rotating earth. Plants were designed to feed the earth's atmosphere with an unending supply of oxygen, *and* fuel and warm the bodies of all life yet to come.

From the beginning of time, God has provided every single thing that humans would need in order to live. He has filled the earth with sound mechanics covered in matchless beauty. But more important than that, He has offered His own Holy Spirit to every single person who chooses to accept His Son, Jesus, as Lord of all.

With the acceptance of Jesus comes salvation, and total forgiveness of sins. Salvation in Christ is only the beginning of life as God wants His beloved to experience it. Jesus opens the door for us to God. It is then, with extreme pleasure, that God pours Himself into our bodies and minds. His Holy Spirit works through each believer to accomplish the will of God.

God has poured out His love into our hearts by the Holy Spirit, Whom He has given us. ROMANS 5:5

With the power of the Holy Spirit, we are given the greatest energy source known to humans. What we choose to do with the power of the Holy Spirit in us determines whether we catapult or crawl through the planning party for our eternal life.

> *Be joyful always; pray continually; give thanks in all circumstances, for this is God's will for you in Christ Jesus. Do not put out the Spirit's fire...* 1 THESSALONIANS 5:16

We can assume that He wasn't just talking to Himself, but to the Holy Spirit that hovered in Him over the waters of the deep, and with the Light, whom we now know as Jesus.

He Knew I Would Tell

My husband, Geoff, and I live in the Midwest, in a mid-sized city and we attend a mid-sized Methodist church called The Turning Pointe, or TTP for short. It's a growing church, full of young families. We had a stretch a few years back with at least one new baby born every month, for twenty-two months running. It's safe to say that there is a lot of love in that church!

A few miles to the west stands a small, picture-perfect, white Methodist church on a country road. About thirty-five people fill the pews each Sunday. The church is relatively quiet, except for the annual fund raising sausage supper, which raises enough money to keep the building in good repair.

Due to the aging population of that little country church, they, as a congregation, decided to merge with our larger church. We planned a celebration to unite the church families at 9:00 on the morning of July 1, 2007.

Our minister asked a few members of our church to go over to the country church for the first united service. He sent his assistant minister to give the sermon, our lead guitar player to accompany their organist, and a handful of our prayer team members to pray before and during the service for blessings on our new church family.

At 8:45 a.m., our minister arrived at the country church to lead us all in a short dedication prayer before he returned to TTP for the 9:00 service there. He invited all who were there to come up front and join us. Altogether, there were probably ten people linked in prayer.

I will never forget that day. I had my right hand on the guitar player's shoulder and my left on the assistant minister's shoulder. The instant our minister opened his mouth to pray, I felt a rush of tingling electricity run from all of my fingertips to all of my toes, through my core body and head. It was wildly shocking, so much so that for a split second I wondered if I was being electrocuted. In the next instant, I knew better. The sensations tickled as they zipped through my body the entire time he prayed, which must have been about three or four minutes. At one point, I opened my eyes ever so slightly to see everyone else's reaction, but the room was calm. Closing my eyes again, I was right back in the middle of what I have since dubbed my *Electric God Moment*. Inside me was a blinding light that felt like neon blue, but had no color that I could describe!

As soon as our minister closed his prayer, the sensation dissipated. He asked another prayer team member to say a short prayer, so I closed my eyes anticipating that the feeling would return, but I was extremely disappointed when it did not. I barely heard her prayer, because I was willing the totally awesome energy back instead. I struggled not to weep when I realized it was gone.

After the prayer session ended, with my hand still on the guitar player, I asked him, "Did you feel that?" He said he didn't feel anything in particular. So I tugged at the assistant minister's arm and asked her, "Did you feel that?" She said "No," but then looked right into my eyes and told me, "but I KNOW". We exchanged a few quick words and a hug, and then she welcomed the rest of the congregation and went on to preach. I sat a few rows back with the other prayer team members and prayed for the united effort of the joining of the congregations, but even more for the return of the spirit that had just filled me so full of indescribable delight.

After the service was over at the country church, I stopped at TTP on my way home. Our minister was standing just inside the door, so I told him what had happened when he spoke. When I finished telling him, he shared that he hadn't felt anything like that as he prayed.

I have had light cases of this before and since this occurrence, as many people have. Around here, we affectionately refer to them as God Bumps. But this time, the intensity of it was off the charts, as was the duration! The timing seemed so intentional. That it was precisely from the beginning to the end of the dedication prayer, and included such total body involvement from head to toe, was all I needed to know that it was The Holy Spirit.

I believe three things about this event. One, the Holy Spirit was with us in that church that day. Two, He was totally loving the uniting of our congregations. Three, somehow I was to be involved at that church.

Soon afterward, I joined two of my friends to lead hymns at that church on scheduled Sundays.

I enjoy sharing this story with anyone who listens. I love to relive it in hopes of inviting the Holy Spirit back for another sensational visit!

I am not the first, and I will not be the last, to experience the wonderful rush of The Holy Spirit's indwelling. Many others have revealed that they, too, have experienced this and have gained knowledge that came wrapped in similar surges of power and love.

Jesus said, *"Return home and tell how much God has done for you."* LUKE 8:39

One day, a friend confronted me after I told her this story. She caught me off-guard when she said, "I'm a good person. I'm a devoted Christian too. Why haven't I ever had anything like this? Why you?"

My brain drew a blank, but my mouth opened up and I replied, "Maybe it's because He knew I would tell."

"But blessed are your eyes because they see, and your ears because they hear. For I tell you the truth, many prophets and righteous men longed to see what you see but did not see it, and to hear what you hear but did not hear it." MATTHEW 13:16

We went on to have a great conversation about sharing God's Word, not only with other Christians, but especially with those who don't yet know Christ as their Savior. We talked about boldly getting His message out there, about how God may have allowed this *Electric God Moment* to happen, so more people would hear it and desire it for themselves. After all, that's what He did when the Jews rejected His Son, Jesus. He turned around and offered eternal life to the Gentiles if they would accept His Son as their Savior. The Jews caught wind of it. Some became jealous enough to start paying attention and claim Him for themselves. Sadly, others had a different reaction.

This *Electric God Moment* was the most fantastic few minutes of my life. It went beyond earthly love as I have ever known it. Far beyond anything I could have dreamed up on my own. Way beyond. And I want more! *Praise God from Whom all blessings flow!*

Jesus answered, "*I was sent only to the lost sheep of Israel.*" *The woman came and knelt before Him. "Lord, help me!" she said. He replied, "It is not right to take the children's bread and toss it to their dogs." "Yes Lord," she said, "but even the dogs eat the crumbs that fall from their masters' table." Then Jesus answered, "Woman, you have great faith! Your request is granted."* MATTHEW 15:24

I felt a rush of tingling electricity run from all of my fingertips to all of my toes, through my core body and head. It was wildly shocking, so much that for a split second, I wondered if I was being electrocuted. In the next instant, I knew better.

Morning Sky

August 12, 2009, 4:15 a.m. I often get up early to write, but this morning I took my coffee outside to watch the Perseid meteor showers instead. The sky was clear and well lit with a bright half moon, plenty of stars, a couple of big shiny planets, and several high flying airliners.

In thirty minutes, I only saw two meteorites, but that was enough time to stroll up the road and have my morning talk with God.

It was hard to keep from gushing on about how beautiful everything looked under the soft glow of the moon. How the white phlox on the side hill looked like a flock of sheep and the spent, closed blossoms of the big hibiscus plant seemed to stand guard behind them, sort of like tired shepherds. A walk down the street brought me to the edge of my neighbor's open field. It appeared quiet, with nothing but a thin layer of fog hovering over the short grass.

By 4:45 that morning, the back woods that separate the neighbor's house from ours began to wake up. I believe I heard the first bird of the day, and then in no time flat, they all seemed to wake up and chime in. It made me wonder what goes on in bird brains. The obvious answer: hungry, find food, feed those noisy kids, clean out the nest, repeat until they finally fly off, look for that mate again, and start all over. Sounds grueling. It emphasizes the blessings bestowed on humans.

Humans seem to have an unlimited capacity to improve their lives. We learn quickly to adapt to our surroundings by making appropriate changes. If we need to get from here to there, we learn how to build a car or an airplane to get us there. Short of that, we learn how to make money so we can pay someone else to build those things, so we can get where we hope to be, without a lot of unnecessary wing flapping.

And that brings us to *hope*, as in *where we hope to be personally with God*. There are so many questions pertaining to hope and God. Here are a few that come to mind: Are you satisfied with your relationship with God? When others talk about how great God is in their life, do you just hope He knows who you are? Does it make you feel inadequate, and worse yet, unloved by this God that people keep holding out all hope for? Do you wonder how people can be so sure that there even is a God?

There are answers to those questions, and so many more, in the Bible. It doesn't matter which version of the Bible you use, but I lean toward the NIV, New International Version, because it's written close to the way I hope to speak. Turn to John 1:1 in the New Testament and read the first two sentences. Read it a few times, then let your mind mull it over.

> *In the beginning was the Word, and the Word was with God, and the Word was God. He was with God in the beginning.*
> JOHN 1:1

The beginning refers to the start of our world, the first moment of time for our universe and all its space. The beginning is when the Spirit of God decided to build something tangible out of nothing.

In the Bible Jesus is referred to as *the Word*. Though He was with God in the beginning, Jesus would eventually be sent to live as a human on earth and express in words what God said on clay tablets and in visions.

Jesus was *with* God and was *part of* the Spirit of God since the beginning of time. Together, they created the heavens and the earth.

Genesis 1:1 records that there was a beginning to planet earth and all that is on it. *In the beginning God created the heavens and the earth. Now the earth was formless and empty, darkness was over the surface of the deep, and the Spirit of God was hovering over the waters.*

Genesis 1:26 explains how we came to look the way we do. *Then God said, "Let us make man in our image, in our likeness..."* Who was God talking to here? What image is God talking about? The Holy Spirit of God and Jesus must have had form by this time. It must have been different from that of the plants and animals they created, because humans, still in the design stage, were created to look like them. And as if that wasn't brilliant enough, the plants and animals that they created first turned out to be the very fuel that would be used to run the bodies of humans!

> *Through Him all things were made; without Him nothing was made that had been made. In Him was life, and that life was the light of men. The light shines in the darkness, but the darkness has not understood it.* JOHN 1:3

Jesus was on the Design Team for the world. What exciting times those must have been! Can you even imagine deciding how different plants would grow from roots or seed into maturity, and be not only beautiful, but useful as far as nutrients and medicine go? The same goes for all things that have been made. How about developing rocks that would reveal brilliant gemstones? Or having a say in the laying of the land to form mountains, valleys, waterfalls, seas and oceans? And what about the other planets, galaxies, and stars, like the sun? And what about water? Oh yes, water! In the whole scheme of life, it's not a trivial thing, that water.

I really enjoy thinking about the beginning of time in this way. To me, life is too well structured, too precise, to have come about by happenstance or some massive explosion where things just sort of fell together correctly.

The life that is the light of men, and that goes for women too, is the very truth that Jesus reveals. His open, honest character teaches us to seek forgiveness for ourselves and then to forgive others who have wronged us. To let it go is to be cleansed, relieved of burdens that weigh heavily on the human mind. Once the weight is lifted, we are able to focus on Him and the tasks Father God gives us to do.

> *Both the One who makes men holy and those who are made holy are of the same family. So Jesus is not ashamed to call them brothers.* HEBREWS 2:11

Sadly, some people never get to the point of accepting Jesus and experiencing His promises of freedom from sin. Many people think they are too far gone to be saved by Him, and they choose to stay in the shadows of their misery. They are the very people Jesus wants to reach, to lift them up and out of the darkness, into the light!

> Jesus said, *"It is not the healthy who need a doctor, but the sick. I have not come to call the righteous, but sinners."* MARK 2:17

There are infinite lessons to learn in the Bible, and they are as relevant today as the day they were written. The Word is alive and hopes to light the pathway to truth for every person. This may take a few minutes for some to understand, or several years for others. Doesn't matter. It is time well spent.

The best way to learn is to start attending a good Bible study. Pass up those that are just social events. Get serious about finding hope and how it belongs in the big plan of life. You will be surprised that there is a lifetime full of tasks already assigned to you! To miss them is to miss out on the opportunities that God has planned for you. He is so awesome — His hope is in you, and He wants you to hope in Him right back!

God is Spirit, and His worshipers must worship in spirit and in truth. JOHN 4:24

Many people think they are too far gone to be saved by Him, and they choose to stay in the shadows of their misery. They are the very people Jesus wants to reach, to lift them up and out of the darkness, into the light!

Speculating On Prayer

The energy that believers around the world share with God runs wide and deep. Many people say that they sometimes see or feel it flow in a variety of colors. They must be the artists among us!

Prayers are like battery charges, but as the weight of the day progresses, the flow may seem to diminish to a thin trickle. You can keep that joyful connection going strong all day with short prayers of thankfulness for all the things that make your life better.

> *And pray in the Spirit on all occasions with all kinds of prayers and requests.* EPHESIANS 6:18

In an average person's day, there is so much to be thankful for. To wake up alert and healthy, that is something to give immediate thanks to God for. If there is food available for breakfast, lunch, and dinner, and a place to call home, so much the better! Praise God for family and friends who share their own variety of love and laughter and add joy to everyday life. When the car starts, or the bus is on time, appointments go as planned, the day runs close to schedule, and the whole family arrives home safe and sound at the end of the day, then that is a blending of many blessings. Phone calls from loved ones, soldiers home from duty, families reunited. It's all worthy of much praise!

> *Give thanks to The Lord, call on His name; make known among the nations what He has done. Sing to Him, sing praise to Him; tell of all His wonderful acts.* PSALM 105:1

Imagine the accumulation of prayers that go to God from individual people around the world.

What might it look like if prayers were visible to us? Would they leave streaks of light? Would the most desperate prayers be punctuated with the thickest, boldest, brightest lights? Might sweet, loving prayers of thankfulness leave contrails of the favorite colors of the person who is praying? Could the air around us be woven with the prayers of God's beloved that have been prayed through the ages?

What path might those prayer lights take as they fly across time zones, continents, oceans, the universe? Would they shoot straight upwards, or out in all directions?

Do all the prayers that are said in all the languages of the world blend together and arrive to God in what we think of as *tongues*?

When prayers reach God's ear, do they then go to a gathering place where that person's other prayers are mixing and building energy for action? Or do they go from God's ear, to His angel helpers, and then right back to the person they are intended for?

> *Are not all angels ministering spirits sent to serve those who will inherit salvation?* HEBREWS 1:14

These are all questions that we will likely learn the answers to when our earthly lives are over.

One more question to ponder: on any given day, what is the ratio of request prayers to thankfulness prayers?

Prayers of thanks must be music to God's ears! Imagine if all you ever heard from your loved ones was one request after another. Imagine how good it must be to hear voices filled with gratefulness and thanks in the midst of all those requests!

> *Sing and make music in your heart to The Lord, always giving thanks to God the Father for everything, in the Name of our Lord Jesus Christ.* EPHESIANS 5:19

Could the air around us be woven with the prayers of God's beloved that have been prayed through the ages?

Meeting God's People

How many times have you met someone and walked away feeling like you have brushed against holiness?

Some people in this world exude God's love. We expect it from a minister, a priest, or a nun. Not that we always get it from them, but it is an expectation. I am talking about sensing an outpouring of love from common, ordinary, everyday people who seem to walk around wrapped in God's blessing.

Some people see auras around other people. I do not. But occasionally I do feel the power of abundant love around people.

I met Marlina Easton during a job interview. She was the third and final candidate for a job opening. The other two people were well qualified and had everything going for them to fill the position. It was going to be a tough decision.

Marlina Easton approached me with a broad smile and her hand outstretched. When we grasped hands, there was a power surge of energy that connected through our palms and eyes. I remember thinking, "Wow! What was that?" We had a good interview. I told her we would call that evening with our decision, one way or the other.

A strong handshake, a broad smile and an intelligent, audible greeting make a very good start to any interview. Marlina had all these things. Her job-securing bonus was the power surge of energy in that handshake.

Two weeks later she phoned me to thank me for the job and asked if we could get together for a cup of coffee. We agreed to meet at a local coffee shop after work the following Friday.

Marlina and I met for coffee once every week or two for years after that. In that time, she skillfully walked me back into Jesus' fold. Years before, I had accepted Jesus, but without a strong foundation under my faith, I had slipped away. The world was alluring, and I never found the time to actually read the Bible that sat on my book shelf in the den. I thought just having it in the house was good enough.

> *The fear of the Lord is the beginning of knowledge, but fools despise wisdom and discipline.* PROVERBS 1:7

Over time, Marlina reintroduced me to Jesus. She made it perfectly clear that she was not going to stop talking until I understood why this was so important.

> *Therefore God exalted Him to the highest place and gave Him the name that is above every name, that at the Name of Jesus every knee should bow, in heaven and on earth and under the earth, and every tongue confess that Jesus Christ is Lord, to the glory of God the Father.* PHILIPPIANS 2:9

In a nutshell, Marlina taught me these fundamental things:

- Jesus is the Son of God.
- Jesus came to earth to teach people what God wanted them to know.
- Jesus forgives who He wants and brings them into God's Family.

- It turns out that Jesus wants and hopes to forgive everyone.
- Each person needs to ask Jesus for forgiveness.
- When a person accepts Jesus, then God Himself gives that person a gift.
- The gift is The Holy Spirit.
- The Holy Spirit is the very essence of God.
- God's Holy Spirit is present and powerful, and lives in each believer.
- The Holy Spirit helps everything He touches turn out for good.
- No one gets to God, or heaven, without accepting Jesus as their Savior.
- No greater love exists than that of Jesus, The Holy Spirit and God.

My purpose is that they may be encouraged in heart and united in love, so that they may have the full riches of complete understanding, in order that they may know the mystery of God, namely, Christ, in Whom are hidden all the treasures of wisdom and knowledge. COLOSSIANS 2:2

Drifting away from God years before had set me up for failure in the most important area of life. I didn't grow my faith. As a matter of fact, for reasons I can't begin to explain rationally I had actually tried to dismantle what little faith was there. But in the corner of my mind was that foolish hope that everything would turn out fine. I thought, "I'm a good person. Sometimes I do good things. Besides, I was saved when I was fourteen. I have a Bible on my bookshelf. It's a given, no Smoking Section for me! I'll get into heaven."

My thinking was crazy. I expected God to come through on an old promise I had made to Him years before, but had broken.

Whoever claims to live in Him must walk as Jesus did. 1 JOHN 2:6

Though I didn't deserve it, through the years Jesus never let me out of His sight.

I thank God every time my friend Marlina comes to mind. There is no doubt that God arranged for us to be friends. I am glad for the day that He sent her on a job interview that eventually brought Jesus back into my life!

You must teach what is in accord with sound doctrine. TITUS 2:1

Whoever claims to live in Him must walk as Jesus did. **1 JOHN 2:6**

Never Alone

by Marlina Easton

Jesus has been my Savior for well over thirty years, and during that time, has also become the Lord of my life. The years have been filled with wonderful blessings, as well as hard times. Fortunately, good health has always been one of His gifts to me. That's probably why this most recent storm has been so pivotal.

I retired from managing a specialty dessert restaurant in late autumn of 2008. Once I was rested, it was obvious that there was so much to do. So many things had been put off over the years. Having plenty of time and energy, I made my plans for the summer, but God gave me more.

It was near the end of May. Winter was finally behind us, and spring was forcing new growth from the earth in Connecticut, where I live. It was a perfect, warm, sunny day to get outside to rake and clear the lawn and garden beds of twigs and leaves.

Before I had barely made a dent in my project, I tripped and fell. I threw out my hands to break the fall. Upon impact, there was a sharp pain in my left wrist.

It took me a few moments to get myself up off the ground. The pain in my wrist seemed to come on gradually, which was a blessing in itself, but it was obvious that I needed medical attention. My niece drove me to the emergency clinic nearby where the technicians cleaned and wrapped my arm as best they could. I returned the next day, while the doctor was at the clinic, and he put a temporary cast on my arm. We scheduled an operation for the following week.

Meanwhile, I carried my new "friend" around with me everywhere. There was pain and stiffness in my arm and fingers. Rubbing seemed like the right thing to do, but the cast got in the way of any relief.

During the operation a week later, a metal plate was placed permanently in my wrist to pull the bones back together again. It was painful coming out of the operation, and the new cast was even more uncomfortable than the first. For several weeks after, my hand and wrist were bound in the cast. At times the pain was extreme. Sleeping became a chore and my waking hours seemed to revolve around figuring out how to do everything without using my arm, or worse yet, without bumping it.

As if that wasn't enough trauma for awhile, within two weeks of the operation, I started getting burning pains in my left leg which made it painful to walk. Years of retail and restaurant work have left me with varicose veins, but this was something new. From the knee down my leg was very red and sensitive, hot to the touch, with visible hard knots. Elevating it helped. I had read about applying a poultice of cayenne red pepper, so I tried it. It actually seemed to help alleviate the pain for long periods of time, so I wrapped some of the poultice in gauze and secured it on the leg from the knee down.

At this point, my left leg was now bandaged, as was my left arm. Maneuvering around the house with one good arm and one good leg was difficult, but not impossible.

A few days had gone by, when I took a fast limp around a

corner and misjudged the space needed to get by. I banged an old injury on my right rib cage right smack into a doorknob. The pain was so extreme that I screamed out loud, and my husband came running. He quickly wrapped my middle section with a wide elastic bandage to give my side some support.

If it didn't hurt so bad, it might be funny. But it did hurt. A lot!

Lying on the couch by day, and in bed at night, wrapped up in gauze bandages, I looked like I'd been hit by a train. Three injuries in less than two weeks had brought my world to a screeching halt.

> Jesus said, "... *And surely I am with you always...*" MATTHEW 28:20

Come to find out, that's exactly where the Lord wanted me to be. I do not for a second believe that He caused any of this pain, but I do believe He used this opportunity to teach me many things that I was too busy to hear before.

> *And we know that in all things God works for the good of those who love Him, who have been called according to His purpose.* ROMANS 8:28

I find it hard to express how much of a comfort my Jesus was during this time of recovery or to explain the peace He brought me. Especially when the medical bills started to arrive! They were astronomical, and each new one that came in the mail nearly put me in a state of shock. I prayed about the bills and felt encouraged to phone the clinic and the hospital to plead my case. I have no health insurance and the bills were going to swallow up much of my retirement savings. Fortunately, after some discussion, the billing department reduced them by half, which was far more reasonable.

The majority of my convalescing time has been spent reading

the Bible and being quiet enough to hear God's precious words to me. They come in whispers and in written word, in song, and in the joy of family and friends as they minister to me. At times during the day, the house is silent enough that I can hear a pin drop. That is when I can hear my Savior's thoughts the clearest, when there are no competing noises to get in the way.

While the couch still cradles my wrapped limbs, I now see how I am a vital part of God's action plan! Jesus has been using this time to teach and assure me that trusting Him and The Holy Spirit for wisdom and knowledge is opening doors so The Father's Will may be done.

I've got this burning fire in my heart to get on with the action plan that Jesus has been showing me. Now, if I could just get up off this couch!

> ... *"My grace is sufficient for you, for my power is made perfect in weakness."* 2 CORINTHIANS 12:9

At times during the day, the house is silent enough that I can hear a pin drop. That is when I can hear my Savior's thoughts the clearest, when there are no competing noises to get in the way.

Campus Crusades

by Cheryl Brown Folz

The summer of 1999, my last real summer as a college student, I went to Brazil on a summer mission project with Campus Crusades for Christ. We spent six weeks on college campuses in Fortaleza. The last week, we went to the smaller city of Natal to do various mission projects and prepared to go back home to the United States.

One of the mission projects that we did in Natal was showing the popular "Jesus" film. Three times that week, we went to very rural areas, set up a movie screen, went around the neighborhood streets and invited people to come see the "Jesus" film in their own native language. The "Jesus" film shares the life and death of Jesus Christ. It has been translated into a thousand languages and is a very effective evangelistic tool used to share Christ's love all over the world.

> *And how can they preach unless they are sent? As it is written, "How beautiful are the feet of those who bring good news!"*
> ROMANS 10:15

As my group of students was on the bus heading to the last "Jesus" film outreach, we were quietly praying for the people who would see the film, that God would touch their hearts.

This could be the first, and maybe the last, time that they might hear about Jesus. I felt led to pray for one individual, and the name Geraldo came to mind. There was no particular reason for that name, it still makes no sense.

We arrived at the last outreach to show the film, walked the streets and invited as many as we could to come and watch it. We had assembled a larger group at that last film than we'd had at all the showings that week. While the film was being shown, I worked behind the scenes with the children. I was not able to see the audience and their reactions during the movie.

When the movie was over, we were visiting with the Brazilians and having fun with the children. A couple of fellow students from my team came to me when they saw I had a camera. They asked if I would take a picture of them with one Brazilian man who had just seen the film, and had asked Jesus to come into his life as a result. While one of my teammates walked off for a few minutes to get something, I talked with the Brazilian man and asked him questions using my broken Portuguese. Finally, I asked his name. His name was Geraldo.

It was beyond words! My teammates did not know about my prayers. When God gave me the name, I prayed for Geraldo, but still in my small mind didn't think there really would *be* a Geraldo. My prayers were used by God to help bring Geraldo to Him. Then, He used my teammates in bringing Geraldo to me, so that I could see how prayer works! I am still (ten years later) incredibly humbled by this experience, it still gives me goose bumps.

One of the mission projects that we did in Natal, was showing the popular "Jesus" film. Three times that week, we went to very rural areas, set up a movie screen, went around the neighborhood streets and invited people to come see the "Jesus" film in their own native language.

Home Again

by Robin Lannert

I hope I never lose that awestruck feeling when I witness God's grace, mercy and provisions at work. But why should I be surprised at the Creator of the universe? Yet I still found myself speechless as I stood, literally on the other side of the world, hugging my little children, tears streaming down my face. Well, I guess they weren't actually *my* children, but they sure felt like my own....

It all had begun two and a half years prior. My husband, Dennis, and I had just come off of a mountain top high. God had blessed us and allowed us the privilege of leading a weekend retreat of over a hundred teens. We had witnessed God perform miracles. We were new Christians, unqualified, and of course, truly unable to pull off such a task on our own. But with God on our side, it was possible.

It was my first day back to work. As I sat, still amazed at God's handiwork, I prayed, "God, thank you for allowing us to serve you this weekend. Now, what do you want from me next? Just let me know because I am *all in*! But God, please make it clear, because you know I have a way of missing hints!" Within an hour of my prayer, my boss walked up to me and randomly asked, "Hey, what's your next spiritual high?"

"I don't know," I replied.

"Well, why don't you go on a mission trip to Myanmar with me?" he asked.

I can't say I saw that one coming! That was certainly clear! I didn't even know where Myanmar was located. In case you don't know either, it is a tiny poverty-stricken, primarily Buddhist country wedged between China, Thailand, and India. But, I had no doubt that God had called me to go.

> (Jesus) *said to them, "Go into all the world and preach the good news to all creation."* MARK 16:15

It was there that I met "my kids." Though there were about two hundred and fifty kids in the orphanage, there were seven orphans that I grew especially close to — four boys and three girls. We laughed, prayed, played, worshipped, sang together, yet barely spoke to one another. Our language was different, but somehow we understood each other. I left Myanmar one week later. My heart was broken. Would I ever see them again? Did they really know that I cared? I didn't know it would hurt so badly to leave.

Two years had passed since I said good-bye to "my kids." Two years is a long time in the lifetime of children. Our bus was pulling onto the orphanage property. I was back. As we pulled onto the grounds, my eyes scanned more than two hundred and fifty Asian-skinned children for familiar faces.

I wanted them to know that I had not forgotten them and that they were loved. Were they still there? Would I recognize them? Would they know me? I stepped off our bus and within seconds I had all seven kids wrapped in my arms. They were taller, but looked the same. They were laughing, saying my name over and over again. Their little arms wrapped so tight around my waist it almost took my breath away. I couldn't believe two years had already gone by. It felt like only yesterday that we had parted. I was crying, unable to utter a word. It was good to be home again. How could I possibly be so blessed?

I learned a lot over those two years. I learned that when you are really ready to follow God's lead, he will clearly direct you with his desires for your life. I have learned that God uses the unqualified to serve his purpose and I have also learned that you just can't out-give God. No matter how determined you are to sacrifice and serve, he always gives you a double dose of blessings. Wow! What an awesome God we serve!

> *I commend to you our sister Pheobe, a servant of the church in Cenchrea. I ask you to receive her in the Lord in a way worthy of the saints and give her any help she may need from you, for she has been a great help to many people, including me.* ROMANS 16:1

I have learned that God uses the unqualified to serve his purpose and I have also learned that you just can't out-give God.

Mimes

I want to share with all of you something that happened at our church that truly speaks to the heart of Christmas. There was not a Santa to be found anywhere, and it went something like this.

The sermon message was called THE GIFT: HOPE. It detailed why Christians can live and die knowing their sins have been forgiven, because of their own personal relationships with God, The Father, His Son, Jesus, and The Holy Spirit.

The lights dimmed and a mime came forward. Yes, that's right, a man sporting white gloves, black slacks and shirt with his face painted white came forward. He showed the congregation his finger with a string tied to it. What could that be for?

A woman came forward and was obviously glad to see him. He showed her the string, but she knew no reason for it either. Then he spotted a big gift box with a note saying it was FROM: GOD. She was curious and wanted to know what was in there. Was it for her? What might God have sent?

The man opened the box and gently reached in and lifted out what looked like a baby bundled in a blanket. She was delighted and took that bundle and cradled and swooned over it. She lifted it high to the heavens as her eyes misted over with love and gratitude. He looked in the box again and pulled out other things: a statue of a woman kneeling down, another of a man standing, with his head bent, looking down. Then, a small baby in a cradle. All these things the man placed on a table for everyone to see.

The woman smiled at the man with that look mothers get when they are loving their child and believe that no one else could ever have known such joy. He smiled back.

The man looked in the box again, and slowly pulled out a small block of wood and placed it on the table. You could almost hear them wondering, "What on earth could that be for?" Then came a hammer and a crude circle of twigs with thorns, but still, neither of them knew why these things were in the gift box from God.

The woman continued to love and nurture her bundle, but her smile seemed to fade as he lifted a wooden cross from the box. It was about two feet high and maybe one foot wide. The man propped the cross on the small block of wood. The final piece he took from the box was a very long nail, about 8 inches long. He looked at the nail with concern and then a look of realization came across his face. He looked at her. She looked back and understood. She tried to hide her bundle from him. He gestured to her with his white-gloved hand to give him the bundle. Tears streamed from her eyes as she shook her head no. You could hear her mind screaming "No! No! No!" but she never said a word. Finally, with deep regret, she handed the bundle over to the man. As she did, the blanket fell away to reveal a large loaf of bread. The bread bore the slash marks of the baker's hand. The man laid the bread on the cross.

The man and woman looked at each other. He pressed the crown of thorns into the top of the bread. He then took the long nail and pierced it through the center of the bread. Taking the hammer in his right hand, and the nail in his left hand, the man pounded the head of the nail, slowly, deliberately, four times. She cringed and wailed silently with hands over her ears, her face streaked with tears. She looked away in horror and shame. Slowly, she walked away. She returned with a goblet of wine. The man dipped the top of the cross in the wine. It was finished.

Together, the man and the woman walked off the altar and stood side by side. She held out the goblet of wine. He held the bread. They offered to every single person in the sanctuary who came forward, to tear off a piece of the bread and dip it in the wine and eat. The body and the blood. The gift: hope. Hope for eternal life in heaven. Jesus already paid the price. He gifted us with His own life. And the string? We need to remember to thank Him for it.

> *"For God so loved the world that He gave His one and only Son, that whoever believes in Him shall not perish, but have eternal life. For God did not send His Son into the world to condemn the world, but to save the world through Him."*
> JOHN 3:16

She was delighted and took that bundle and cradled and swooned over it. She lifted it high to the heavens as her eyes misted over with love and gratitude.

Welcome Home

by Vicki Brasel

I wonder just how many times I have missed the footsteps of God. As I look back I can see that I was not prepared for, nor even looking for, His footsteps. What a shame. The Creator of the universe loves each of us so much that He takes time to arrange personal *God moments*, yet we miss so many of them.

After a couple of years of pursuing God with all my heart, studying and applying His Word, I began to see life more clearly. It was then that I recognized my first personal *God moment*. Since that time I have been blessed to have had several of them, and am so thankful now to recognize them as the gifts they are meant to be.

In retrospect, I can see how my Heavenly Father started putting everything in place for that one special moment, or as I call it, "for such a time as this". No matter how many *God moments* I now recognize, I stand in total amazement each and every time. They never lose any value or power; after all, they are just for me from my Creator.

Now faith is being sure of what we hope for and certain of what we do not see. HEBREWS 11:1

One that I will share with you happened at Christmas. First, I must tell you that the prior year God had arranged a very special *God moment* about my mother who had passed away a few years before. So, this is my second *God moment* that included my mother at Christmastime!

Some years I put all of my Christmas decorations out, and some years I don't. Living by myself, especially if I am not planning to be home much during the holidays, it's sometimes best to display a few favorite holiday things, and leave it at that.

This one particular year, I toyed with the idea of decorating minimally. However, wanting to find just the right few decorations, I pulled every box that was marked *Christmas* out of storage and into the living room.

Sitting on the floor, with soft Christmas music playing, I started to carefully unwrap each individual ornament. I remember thinking at the time that I should be doing this with someone.

There was a bag with a logo that said *Welcome Home*. Inside it was a box that was marked "crystal candle holders". I thought to myself, "I don't remember these, nor would it be a style I would have bought". As I lifted the lid of the box I saw FOR VICKI written in my mother's handwriting. Inside the box were two little white angels. I never remember seeing these angels the years before when I had gone through all the ornaments, nor could I remember the box with my name on it.

I started to wonder: what is the significance of *Welcome Home?* Was I going to die soon and be with my mother in heaven? Or was it a reminder that she is in heaven? Needless to say, I had so many tears of joy as I started thinking back about everything God had arranged for me for this moment. I was elated, and with my face on the floor went into prayers of thanks. Thank you hardly seemed appropriate.

Thinking back, I have to ask, how long ago were the angels purchased? Why did she label the box that way? How did the bag, from a store I never shopped at, get into my ornament storage box? Where was this box prior to the night I opened it? I believe that God had put it all in order for His perfect time.

That same evening, I had plans to attend the annual Christmas program at my church. Looking back, it may have been because I was still knee-deep in ornaments, but I changed my mind and decided not to go. Decorations had taken over the living room, and I really wanted to pull it all together before the day ended.

Not wanting to miss out on the joy garnered from attending a Christmas program, I decided to attend one at another local church the next evening. It would be a nice way to end the weekend.

It was a fine presentation, and in it was a message. The message was about how Mary and Joseph went home to register for the census, and, of course, that was at the same time that Jesus was born. The minister said that people have been going home for Christmas for a long time. He went on to say how great it is to be home at Christmas, but then he reminded all believers that it isn't our real home. Home is asking God into your heart and living for Him. *That home* brings us to the threshold of our heavenly home, even as we live here on earth.

I looked down at the bulletin in my hands and saw that the title was *Welcome Home*, and then the choir sang the song *Coming Home to Christ*. It was a song not about death, but life!

The *Welcome Home* bag with the two angels in it flashed through my mind and took on a fresh, new meaning. I sat there with tears of joy streaming down my face. To me it was a message from God, and from my mother in heaven, saying to me *Welcome Home*! It was an affirmation from God of where I was in my walk with Him, and that my mother was seeing my journey from her home in heaven. I gained great comfort from knowing that this would greatly bless my mother's spirit.

During my mother's lifetime, all she ever saw from me were the rituals of following a religion. She had comfort in knowing that I knew Jesus as my Savior, and I attended Sunday services, but that was the extent of my faith life. My faith had no depth. I did not share the same hunger for God's truth and love that she always prayed I would.

Now I believe that God has shown my mother that her prayers are being answered. I believe she now sees me as a faithful believer in the salvation that comes from knowing Jesus Christ as Lord. The Holy Spirit is enriching my spirit life with the knowledge, wisdom and understanding that comes from studying and applying The Word of God to life. The result is the building of a very real and deeply personal relationship with Him. I am so blessed to feel that she has insight to that.

> *But the wisdom that comes from heaven is first of all pure; then peace-loving, considerate, submissive, full of mercy and good fruit, impartial and sincere.* JAMES 3:17

After the Christmas program, I called one of my sisters to tell her. She loves and believes in The Lord also. I am not judging her, but the skepticism that she greeted my *God moment* with encouraged me to pray for the growth her faith. Quite likely, this was the same prayer that our mother had said for each of us in the past.

My sincere prayer is that my sister will grow to know and love God as her own *Father God*, who loves her beyond any human measure. She already knows and accepts that He sent His Son Jesus as a ransom for our sins, but my prayer is that the depth of that critical sacrifice would reveal to her our Father God's eternal intentions for the rest of His family. I pray she realizes that Jesus is alive and is actively calling and gathering each soul to Himself for redemption, so the family of God can get on with the details of His Will to be done. I pray that she understands the magnitude of what it means when God honors all who believe in His Son, by sending the very essence of Himself to them in the gift of The Holy Spirit. Once He is given by Father God, The Holy Spirit lives in every single believer and reveals Scriptural knowledge to all who seriously inquire.

… God has poured out His love into our hearts by the Holy Spirit, whom He has given us. ROMANS 5:5

My prayer continues that my sister would find herself in the position to recognize and accept the special *God moments* as He presents them to her. That she would know that it is fine and acceptable to look for His presence in the details of her life. And that His presence will take different forms, for different people, at different times. Our God is not boring! He delights in surprising His children.

I don't believe in coincidences, and I don't try to make things up, but I know God can use boxes, bags, angels, Christmas programs and people to send his personal messages to us. Get yourself in a position to be ready to receive them, because that night as I unwrapped that bag, that box and those ornaments, the Holy Spirit was speaking to me with a personal message from God, and He will speak to you also.

While Peter was still speaking these words, The Holy Spirit came on all who heard the message. ACTS 10:44

It was a song not about death, but life!

"Do Miracles Still Happen?"

My eleven-year-old nephew asked this question one day while we were talking about God.

"Yes, miracles still happen today." I replied. "The problem is, God gives us so many, that we take them for granted. Sometimes, we end up brushing them off as coincidences. On top of that, unless a situation happens to us personally, it usually doesn't stay lodged in our memory for long."

Earlier that same day, I had read of a miracle connected with the second Gulf War. I shared it with my nephew, and it went like this: It was early in the war, our troops on the ground had formed a long convoy and were driving across the desert when a big windstorm blew up. The media reported it as "a one hundred year storm". The convoy was forced to stop and hunker down in their vehicles for several hours. When the storm passed, the soldiers emerged from their vehicles to see that many land mines were exposed on the sandy road in front of them.

The strong winds had uncovered the mines. Our troops were saved by the one hundred year storm. That's a miracle!

The book of Hebrews was written to the second generation of Christians to remind them again of the salvation that comes only from Jesus, and of the miracles He performed while on earth. This was to encourage them to continue to grow their faith.

> *... This salvation, which was first announced by the Lord, was confirmed to us by those who heard Him. God also testified to it by signs, wonders and various miracles, and gifts of the Holy Spirit distributed according to His will.* HEBREWS 2:3

On January 15, 2009, at 3:30 p.m., another public miracle happened. An Airbus A320 had just taken off from LaGuardia Airport in New York, headed to Charlotte, North Carolina. A flock of geese got caught in the engines, causing one of them to catch on fire, and both to fail. The pilot, Captain Chelsey "Sully" Sullenberger, and his co-pilot, First Officer Jeff Skiles, had approximately three minutes to impact, so they located the closest landing area and skillfully turned the plane toward it. They worked diligently to make it a smooth landing. Ninety seconds before impact, the Captain notified the passengers and crew to brace for impact. People phoned loved ones and others prayed. Captain Sully and First Officer Skiles landed the airbus smoothly and safely on the waters of the Hudson River, saving all one hundred and fifty-five lives on board. Rescue vessels approached immediately and escorted every single person to shore safely.

Quick thinking by the skilled pilot and co-pilot, along with an airbus full of prayers, including those of people watching from the shore and rescue vessels, made for a miraculous, safe landing.

> *But the eyes of the Lord are on those who fear Him, on those whose hope is in His unfailing love, to deliver them from death and keep them alive in famine.* PSALM 33:18

The media reported it as "a one hundred year storm". The convoy was forced to stop and hunker down in their vehicles for several hours.

Even Tough Marines Love Jesus

by Phil Young & Cheryl Mochau

Camp Lejuene is always looking for a few good men. The very sound of the name, Camp Lejuene, rolls off the tongue with an exotic flair. My brothers, sister and I had fun repeating the name over and over. Our older brother Phil and three other friends had enlisted in the Marine Corps together, and would soon be going to Paris Island for boot camp and then to Camp Lejuene for infantry training. Being immature, we did not understand that basic training was necessary to teach them to fight and survive a war in some far off country halfway around the world, in a place called Viet Nam. Ignorance is bliss.

The young men were pumped and ready to go. It was the first time any of them had ever flown in an aircraft. The promise of a free college education after the war fueled their ambitions.

At 3 a.m. on March 19, 1969, Phil came in from his usual night patrol. It was pitch dark and he took his first watch as they settled into the mud and thick, heavy grass on the bank of the river to watch for enemy activity. He sat his watch while occasional rounds came in from the enemy as a form of harassment. He did not know of the major battle that was about to be sprung from the village of Hiep Duc, directly across the river. It had always been a hotbed of Viet Cong activity. Just upstream was Liberty Bridge, and the firebase on Hill 37, his home base.

At 4 a.m. Phil was relieved from duty and told to get some much-needed sleep. Marine grunts covet every minute of sleep they can get so he didn't waste any time falling asleep right where he was positioned in the mud and tall grass on the river bank.

Shortly after Phil dozed off, the Viet Cong and their northern brothers (NVA) effectively breached the perimeter, which was heavily strung with razor wire. They broke through the wire at several points and attacked the sleeping post. Thunderous chaos engulfed the tiny post as the enemy attacked with a barrage of fire including rockets, mortars, grenades and small arms. Phil was shot in the front of the throat with a single round from an AK-47 rifle. The bullet flipped as it as it passed through his neck, severing the right subclavian artery and vein and the mammary artery, lodging in the heavy muscle of his back under his right shoulder blade. As it passed through, it destroyed the upper lobe of his right lung. He remembers waking up slapping the entry hole thinking he had been stung by a bee.

His fellow Marines of Alpha Company, 1st Battalion, 7th Marines, 1st Division sprang into action for three hours of fierce fighting, some of it hand-to-hand.

Meanwhile, Liberty Bridge and his home base, Hill 37, were being hit simultaneously. The Marines held their ground and the larger battle lasted all day.

Phil owes his life to the skill of the Corpsman, and his fellow Marines, both on the ground and those brave chopper crews who got him out, despite the heavy fire they took during his rescue. He is alive today because everyone did their job and did it well. Timing is everything. Phil also knows he could not have survived without his being watched over by a greater power!

No matter what Hollywood does to glamorize war, in real time, it's ugly and hard and hellish.

During the Viet Nam war, tragedies like Phil's were reported to the families back home by Western Union telegram. My brother Bob got the news first. It bluntly stated that our brother was wounded and was currently recovering in a Naval Hospital in Da Nang. They had operated on him and he was partially paralyzed. They would keep us informed of his progress.

After school that day, my siblings and I barged into the house with the usual noise of four kids who were glad to be home. Our brother Bob was sitting quietly in his favorite chair in the living room. Without a word he held out the paper for us to see. We stared at the telegram in quiet disbelief. Bad news like that shocks the human body.

This was hard news to take. Phil was handsome, smart, strong, and full of life when we last saw him. Now this yellow sheet of paper spelled out that he was lying on a hospital bed in some place called Da Nang, gravely wounded. We were numb.

Word of Phil's brush with death spread through the tiny towns where he had made sports headlines in high school. Calls came in to our family that people from all over the region were praying for him. People stopped by to bring hope and tell us in person that their churches were praying for Phil's recovery.

> ... *The Lord is near. Do not be anxious about anything, but in everything, by prayer and petition, with thanksgiving, present your requests to God.* PHILIPPIANS 4:5

Phil was eventually transferred to St. Albans Naval Hospital in Queens, New York, where he fought hard to regain mobility and regain the use of his right arm. He learned to walk, talk and write all over again. His first letters home, written in his own hand, were crushing to read. They were written in the scrawl of a five year old, but with the sentiment of one now far older than his nineteen years.

By God's grace, Phil recovered from his war wounds. In fact, all four of the young men that joined the Marines together returned home from the war.

Phil became an advocate for other veterans who needed help overcoming the haunting shock of war. To this day, he counsels young patriots who are stationed in war zones all over the world.

In the process of helping others, Phil reconnected with, and grew, his own faith in God. With the steadfast teaching of his close friend, Father Tom Stott, Phil came to understand and use the power that is behind prayer. He learned that it was the outpouring of prayers from family, friends and congregations of the faithful that brought his broken body before God for mercy and healing in his greatest hours of need. Now he does the same for others.

> *Blessed is the man who finds wisdom, the man who gains understanding...* PROVERBS 3:13

Interestingly, Father Stott was a Naval Corpsman attached to the 7th Marines. He and Phil did not know each other during the war, as they were assigned to different companies, but met each other at college after they returned home. Father Stott was a good friend of the Corpsman that saved Phil's life that night.

God's grace softened Phil's heart and led him to understand and accept Jesus in his life. Even the toughest Marines love Jesus.

... It is by the Name of Jesus Christ of Nazareth, Whom you crucified but Whom God raised from the dead, that this man stands before you healed. ACTS 4:10

He learned that it was the outpouring of prayers from family, friends and congregations of the faithful that brought his broken body before God for mercy and healing in his greatest hours of need.

The Little Lung That Could

by Christa Shore

After ten months on oxygen and nearly nine months on the waiting list, my husband, Mike, at age 47, received The Gift of Life on Sunday, January 4, 2009, in the earliest hours of the morning.

God answered our long awaited prayers with the gift of a new lung, breath, extended life for Mike and time for all of us who love him. Praise be to God for His awesome works! All glory to Him for the miracle of life!

We received "The Call" at 6:13 in the morning, on Saturday, January 3rd, from our transplant coordinator at Methodist Hospital in Indianapolis saying "Mike, we have a set of lungs for you! We need you to come as quickly as possible." We were on the road to Indy at 6:30 a.m., and at Methodist Hospital by 10:00 a.m.

> ... Jesus said to Jairus, "Don't be afraid; just believe, and she will be healed." LUKE 8:50

They prepped Mike for surgery immediately, but due to a delay in placing the donor heart, surgery actually began that evening around 8:30 p.m. As Dr. Fehrenbacher and his surgical team opened Mike's right side to begin the process of removing his right lung, Dr. Wozniak and his team were in Nebraska retrieving a set of lungs from a young organ donor.

As the organ retrieval team was flying back with a new set of lungs for Mike, the surgical team was running into some complications. Mike's right lung had been biopsied three and a half years previously and due to his disease process, his body had completely and relentlessly adhered the diseased lung to his chest wall in such a horrific manner that the dissection of the right lung that would normally have taken thirty minutes took over two hours to complete. Once opened the team could see that Mike's chest cavity was much deeper than they had anticipated.

The donor lungs arrived on time, but though the right lung was perfect, the left lung had become damaged during the retrieval process.

Unfortunately, the donor lungs were much too small, and an awkward anatomical match for Mike.

The surgical team decided because the left lung wasn't viable and the right was so small, Mike's chance for survival and quality of life would be grossly compromised if they used the small right lung. They made the difficult decision to close his chest, keep him in Critical Care on life support and aggressively search for another set of lungs immediately.

Dr. Wozniak came to give our family the tragic news. I asked why the decision was made. Dr. Wozniak humbly explained how he had personally gone to Nebraska to retrieve these specific lungs for Mike. He said he knew how hard Mike had worked, and that he was a very active man, so they had tried everything they could to preserve his quality of life. I responded to Dr. Wozniak, "I know you have Mike's best interest mind. I trust your judgment. Do whatever is best."

Mike's nurse said, "I'm sorry, this went so wrong. It was not at all as we had planned and hoped. I don't even know what to say."

Our family was in shock. We knew we would most probably lose Mike. There is no way to adequately convey the surreal disappointment, anxiety and fear we experienced during those hours. We were devastated beyond belief.

As Dr. Fehrenbacher finished closing Mike's chest and they began to send Mike to Cardio-Vascular Critical Care [CVCC], the surgeon changed his mind. Feeling it was Mike's only chance for survival, Dr. Fehrenbacher called Dr. Wozniak, who had already gone home, to come back, re-open and place the small lung into Mike's chest.

They informed us of the new decision. We were ambivalent. We knew Mike's chance for a normal quality of life would be compromised. He would be so disappointed. The discussion of finding a left lung would mean using a second donor. And that would mean a much greater chance for rejection. But they felt the risk would outweigh his slim chance of survival otherwise. We feared Mike's response.

We waited. The entire surgery took approximately seven hours. That's two hours over the normal five hour time frame to replace two lungs. At 3:30 a.m., Mike was wheeled into CVCC for recovery.

Dr. Fehrenbacher came to explain to us the difficulties of this unusual surgery, the possible prognosis and options for attempting to provide Mike with a quality of life. He and Mike's transplant Pulmonologist, Dr. Reynolds, then met to discuss Mike's difficult and unusual case and make vital decisions early that morning. They hoped to find a left lung of a larger size to replace the diseased lung that remained in Mike's left side. That would mean starting the wait time again, and waiting for yet another call, but with much less chance of survival and a much lower quality of life from here on out. What cost? In the meantime they watched and waited to see how he would respond to the small right lung — and so did we.

Beyond all our highest expectations — the little right lung took to Mike's body as if it were his own from the start. By 10:00 the morning of the surgery, Mike was taken off the ventilator, and then two hours later he was off all oxygen. This was incredible! No transplant recipient goes off oxygen before leaving CVCC, and many even go home on oxygen for a time after a two-week to three-week stay.

> *Then Jesus said to the centurion, "Go! It will be done just as you believed it would." And His servant was healed at that very hour.* MATTHEW 8:13

Mike was breathing one-hundred-percent on his own. His blood oxygen saturation levels were also one-hundred-percent. This again was incredible! His doctors were in awe!

Within a few hours after surgery he stood, walked, ate a light meal and spoke to us coherently. Incredible! Normally a transplant recipient stays in CVCC from three to five days, and only stands up the last day there. No one had ever walked the day of surgery before. But Mike was beating all the previously set records, and all on that one little lung.

People were coming by to be encouraged by Mike, shaking their heads, laughing, crying with joy at this miracle before us. We named his lung "The Little Lung That Could". He was released from CVCC and placed in his own room on the organ transplant "life & death" floor - 7 North - within thirty-six hours. Amazing!

The doctors and staff, along with all of us, were amazed over and over at what we were seeing. What should never have happened — did. He was breathing and functioning better and more quickly than most double lung transplant patients, better than any of his doctors and nurses could have anticipated. By day two, he was up and walking around the transplant unit with unbelievable results!

God gave us the miracle we prayed for so fervently for three-and-a-half years.

Mike walked, ate, passed all the tests and did so well in his first few days on the transplant unit that he was scheduled to go home on Friday, only five days after lung transplant surgery. Ordinarily, that would require a two-week to three-week hospital stay. His painful chest tubes came out on Thursday, so his pain began to subside greatly.

But we weren't finished yet...

That Tuesday, January 6th, my mom became very ill, fell, aspirated and nearly died. My dad found her. She was taken by ambulance to our local hospital ER and admitted to the Critical Care Unit for five days. She then went to a room, relapsed, and only then was finally stable enough to go home after eight days in the hospital. She was weak for awhile, but stable, and was resting at home, with care from my dad.

> When Paul pleaded with Jesus to remove the thorn from his flesh, Jesus told him, "... *My grace is sufficient for you, for my power is made perfect in weakness.*" 2 CORINTHIANS 12:9

Friday, January 9th, the day we were scheduled to come home, Mike began having extreme labor-type cramps with vomiting and diarrhea that lasted for several days, though they tried everything to stop it. He became delirious, hallucinating and was psychotic all day and night from the immunosuppressant medications. He was so dehydrated they couldn't draw blood, so an emergency procedure to insert a pic line in his arm was performed in his room. Then a naso-gastric [NG] tube with suction was inserted into his stomach to keep him from aspirating, which would have been a potentially fatal complication.

When I asked Dr. Reynolds what this could be, he replied, "We don't know, just don't know."

An emergency CT scan was done at midnight in hopes to find a cause. The lung looked clean. After many tests over the next few days it was finally determined that it was a gastric condition caused either by a viral infection, or most probably one related to his medications. They made some adjustments in his immunosuppressant medications, and after five days his nausea and cramping subsided, and the NG tube was removed. Mike slept most of that week.

Friday, January 16th, Dr. Reynolds, Mike's transplant Pulmonologist, performed a scheduled bronchoscopy to look inside Mike's new lung, do a biopsy and also remove some sloughing tissue that had formed at the bronchial graft obstructing his breathing. Mike felt great after the procedure and could breathe better than he had ever before! He could begin to imagine leading a normal active life again!

After the bronchoscopy procedure, they wanted to watch him over the weekend, so we prepared to come home on Monday, January 19th, just over two weeks post-surgery.

We knew weren't out of the woods yet when another life threatening complication occurred. Mike's Saturday morning X-ray showed that his new lung was collapsing. Thirty percent of the air that should have been inside his lung was leaking into his chest cavity. An emergency procedure was quickly performed: the insertion of a chest tube with suction. This was another unusual set-back.

Daily X-rays and CT scans showed continued leakage of air, so the painful chest tube had to remain in place. But even so, Mike walked daily.

His oxygen was between 96% and 100%, which is great for a person with two healthy lungs. Although a small amount of air remained around the new lung, Dr. Reynolds felt sure the leak had sealed so the chest tube was removed.

Tests showed that on Thursday, January 22nd, his lung seemed to have completely inflated to fit his chest cavity! He took his six minute walk and beat the standing record of fourteen-hundred feet in six minutes by a double lung transplant patient — *Mike walked seventeen-hundred and eighty feet in six minutes with blood oxygen saturation levels of ninety-six with one lung!* Mike was released and we arrived home that same night.

> *Jesus said, "… Your faith has healed you. Go in peace."* LUKE 8:48

Mike was restricted to our home, and unable to have visitors for the first few weeks after his surgery, because of the great risk of picking up germs or viruses due to immunosuppression. What would be a small cold to us would be life-threatening to him.

The past year since the surgery has been extremely exhausting, but at the same time we continue to remain amazed at "The Little Lung that Could", and our "Big God Who Can", whom we've trusted through this entire three-and-a-half year process.

We are humbly grateful to the incredible team of physicians, nurses and staff who have held up Mike's health and our spirits throughout his surgery and recovery.

We are also humbly grateful to our beloved family and friends who have prayed, encouraged and helped us through this entire process. We love and appreciate all of them so much!

We will never be able to express the gratitude we feel toward the family of the person who generously gave Mike back to us. We continue to pray for their family and friends as they grieve the unbearable loss of the one they love so dearly. Through them, and by God's provision, Mike received Life.

Mike's body has responded well to his new lung, far beyond the expectations of any of his doctors, nurses and staff. Though there have been set-backs, we all remain amazed at this incredible miracle of Life we've watched unfold before our eyes! Every day of Life is such a gift. Blessed be The Name of the Lord!

Thanks be to God for His indescribable gift! 2 CORINTHIANS 9:15

People were coming by to be encouraged by Mike, shaking their heads, laughing, crying with joy at this miracle before us.

Praise for Miracles of Today

by Peggy Shorter & Cheryl Mochau

My brother, Jerry, had been sick for quite awhile. He had gotten so sick, in fact, that our family had been preparing to make the long trip to see him, for what we thought would be *the final visit.*

It was a Thursday when the call came from his wife that Jerry had been taken by ambulance to the emergency room at their local hospital. We knew it was time to drop everything and go.

As we drove north, my husband, Gary, and I prayed for Jerry's recovery, and for God's will in his life.

> *"But seek first His kingdom and His righteousness, and all these things will be given to you as well."* MATTHEW 6:33

At the hospital, we found that Jerry was dehydrated and both kidneys were shutting down. He was comatose and on life support, breathing through a ventilator, while his blood was being cleansed of toxins by dialysis. Jerry had a serious staph infection, bleeding in the stomach, jaundice, and pneumonia. It didn't look good for him.

As our family members gathered around Jerry's bed, we prayed, each in our own way, for Jerry's recovery.

God saw fit to use this desperate moment in our family's life to breathe healing onto Jerry.

> ... *"According to your faith will it be done to you"* MATTHEW 9:29

Within two days, Jerry showed remarkable improvement. The color came back into his skin and he was able to breathe on his own. When he spoke, he knew what he wanted. As soon as he could, Jerry asked for a cup of coffee and said he wanted to go home!

Suffice it to say, we were all surprised! So were Jerry's doctor and his attending nurses. They called his recovery a miracle! Jerry had not been expected to leave the hospital alive.

On Sunday, they moved him out of the intensive care unit and assigned him a room on the recovery floor. Just two days later, Jerry was on his way to the local rehab hospital, where he finished his recovery a week later.

Jerry's ten day ordeal in the hospital ended well. Both his kidneys have since been declared fine, and he has no more need for any dialysis. Jerry, who just ten days before was at death's door, was sent home to live life instead.

Praise God for the miracle of healing Jerry, because that's what we believe he is — a walking miracle!

> *Indeed he was ill, and almost died. But God had mercy on him, and not on him only but also on me, to spare me sorrow upon sorrow.* PHILLIPPIANS 2:27

They called his recovery a miracle! Jerry had not been expected to leave the hospital alive.

Crushed, But Not Destroyed

The power of prayer from a couple of strangers, mixed with some very good medical care, restores a broken man to good health, inside and out.

Diane's son, Joe, is in his late thirties. He is a recently divorced tradesman who struggles with drug and alcohol addictions. He was finally beginning to get ahead financially, so he bought a motorcycle. As far as motorcycles go, it was a beauty! Long story short, Joe took the motorcycle out for its first run and accidentally crashed it into a telephone pole on a busy city street.

Joe was knocked unconscious. He lay crushed and broken on the side of the street along with his motorcycle. His skull was crushed and his back was broken.

At the hospital the doctors told Joe's family that he would most likely be paralyzed from the neck down, probably for life. His mother gave him the horrible news when he finally woke up. Together they cried over the severity of the situation.

Friends of Diane heard the news and went to the hospital to pray with Joe. At one point, when one of her friends and Joe were alone in the hospital room, he confided in the woman that he was afraid. He said he was afraid of everything, including life in a wheelchair, but even more afraid of death.

These two strangers shared a vulnerable moment of grief. God used that private time to bring Joe to the realization that life was empty and frightening without Christ.

> *"... Whoever believes in the Son has eternal life, but whoever rejects the Son will not see life, for God's wrath remains on him." JOHN 3:36*

It wasn't but a month later when Joe walked, very slowly, into his mother's church on his own two feet. He was surrounded by well wishers, and his mother's praying friends were among them. They knew answered prayer when they saw it. Joe did too. Joe is on the mend now, physically and spiritually. It hasn't been easy for him to break the cycle of sin that has gripped his life through the years. Joe is seeking God and attends church whenever he is able.

> *So from now on we regard no one from a worldly point of view. Though we once regarded Christ in this way, we do so no longer. Therefore, if anyone is in Christ, he is a new creation; the old has gone, the new has come! 2 CORINTHIANS 5:16*

God used that private time to bring Joe to the realization that life was empty and frightening without Christ.

Everything Will Be Alright

by Sandy Berlin as told to Cheryl Mochau

Charlie and Sandy Berlin had a good life together. They met when they were teenagers, eventually married and had children. They each had successful careers, he as a captain and detective on the local police force and she as a hairdresser. They loved to travel, often driving to Florida to spend time with Sandy's sister and her family. They took local and long trips on their touring motorcycle, and enjoyed relaxing on a Caribbean cruise as well as on the beaches of the Hawaiian Islands.

Charlie and Sandy enjoyed sharing time with their grandchildren. Being tall and strong, Charlie liked to rough house with the grandchildren. It was during one of those playtimes that Sandy looked out the window and saw Charlie resting while the children played all around him. He looked tired. Later that evening, Sandy voiced her concern and suggested he go see a doctor. Having just had a routine physical, he put it off for awhile. But before long, Charlie noticed random episodes of tiredness and shortness of breath, so he made an appointment.

The same day of his doctor's visit, Charlie was looking forward to coming home and taking his wife out for a pizza. Charlie was a big guy with a good appetite, and he burned off his calories as quickly as he took them in. He enjoyed food.

The doctor himself phoned their home around five o'clock and Sandy answered. At the same time, she could hear the garage door opening, so she asked the doctor to hold on while Charlie made his way to the phone.

Charlie picked up the phone nearest the front door, and Sandy stayed on the line to hear what the doctor had to say. After all, when it comes to medical terminology, two heads are better than one.

The doctor greeted Charlie and said, "Charlie, your white blood count is low. I'd like you to swing by the hospital tonight for another test."

Charlie told him he was planning on taking Sandy out for a pizza and he would be there tomorrow. The doctor pushed him to come right away, and again Charlie voiced his choice for a pizza. Finally, Sandy got the message, and motioned to Charlie that he had better go to the hospital that night. So, they did.

Leukemia is a disease of the blood, and Charlie had it. He was admitted to the hospital and put through a course of chemotherapy. After testing, it showed that he still had a low white blood count. They put him through a second course of the treatment. The two of them stayed confined to a private hospital room from January through March. To avoid contamination, they had all their food brought in from the cafeteria. Their laundry was sent out and decontaminated before it was allowed back in the room. During those months, Charlie never once left the room. Sandy left rarely. Visitors were limited, and anyone who came in needed to be completely covered in a gown and mask. Even plants and flowers sent to cheer them were not allowed in the closed room, for fear of contamination.

Visitors could come and see them through the window. They

phoned in and had conversations. One steady visitor was a friend Charlie had made when he made rounds while on the police force. The man was a Christian who took it upon himself to help Charlie have a closer walk with Jesus. They would talk on the phone while looking up scripture in their Bibles. It was a great time of spiritual growth for both Charlie and Sandy.

In the solitude of their hospital room, Charlie and Sandy grew even closer as a couple. They talked about everything under the sun. They read and studied the scriptures that Charlie's friend shared with them.

Through the years, neither Charlie nor Sandy had gone to church much, but both knew God and Jesus. Through their conversations, they found it interesting that both of their mothers had told them that when they were mature enough to make the decision for themselves, they should be baptized.

On one of the rare nights that Sandy did not sleep over in the hospital room, Charlie had a visitor. First thing in the morning he called Sandy to tell her about it. He said, "You're not going to believe what happened. You're going to think I've lost my mind, but it was real. A man was standing right there." Charlie pointed to the exact spot next to his bed. He went on to explain, "I don't know who it was. Maybe it was God, or Jesus. I don't know. But he told me things, without using actual words. He communicated to me that if I did what he said, then everything would be alright. He reached toward me and told me to take his hand, so I did. His hand was so warm! Instantly I was filled with warmth that I can only describe as love. I have never felt anything like that before. He told me that I have a purpose in this life and if I did what he said, then everything would be alright. I asked him what my purpose was. He didn't give any details, but again communicated to me that if I did what he said, then everything would be alright."

Sandy listened wide-eyed. She told Charlie, "I believe you. I do." She thought to herself how in all their years together

Charlie had never lied to her. If he said it happened, then she believed him.

> *… Jesus Himself stood among them and said to them, "Peace be with you." They were startled and frightened, thinking they saw a ghost.* LUKE 24:36

During the three months of confined treatment, Charlie and Sandy had plenty of time to rehash that night-time visit. They talked about it and wondered about it. They surmised that the words "everything will be alright" meant that Charlie would live. They clung to that thought and believed that he would.

Sandy believes that at one point during the long hospital stay, she too had a spiritual visitor. She recounts sitting on the couch in the hospital room, hunched over, deep in a state of worry. It was as if someone came close and wrapped her in a warm blanket for a very brief time. Sandy never saw anyone, but she gained strength and comfort from the unexpected sensation of love.

That summer, Charlie convalesced at home. Sandy cared for him the whole time. In early July, he took his last chemotherapy treatment. It did not raise his white blood count as they had hoped, and the doctors sent him home. Charlie told Sandy that he was feeling better than he had in a while. To her surprise, Charlie suggested that they take a trip to Florida.

He asked her to call her sister and see if it would be a convenient time for a visit, and if there was room to stay with them. They, too, were shocked that Charlie felt well enough to travel. Sandy had her doubts that he was strong enough for such a long drive, but he insisted, so off they went, with Charlie at the wheel.

While visiting their family in Florida, Charlie enjoyed doing everything they usually did with a few precautions. At the pool, he chose a spot in the shade. When they went out to eat, he ate a little less than usual, and maybe just a bit slower. They had a great visit. When Charlie began to show signs of fatigue, they headed for home.

Charlie drove most of the thousand miles home, except for about two hundred of it when he relinquished the driving to Sandy. Charlie had always been her provider and protector, and in his mind, that had not changed.

As the miles flew by, they talked about what their next move would be. The detective in him worked over the nagging question, "What's my purpose?" After much discussion, Charlie announced that he wanted to be baptized. Sandy agreed that she, too, would like to be baptized.

> *Then Jesus came to them and said, "All authority in heaven and on earth has been given to Me. Therefore go and make disciples of all nations, baptizing them in the name of the Father and of the Son and of the Holy Spirit, and teaching them to obey everything I have commanded you. And surely I am with you always, to the very end of the age."* MATTHEW 28:18

Upon arriving home, Charlie phoned his Christian friend and told him of their decision to be baptized. The friend was delighted and offered to make all the arrangements at his church.

The following Sunday, Charlie and Sandy arrived at the church early. They were given a set of clothes to wear for the full immersion baptism. Sandy entered the baptismal area first, and carefully walked the few steps down into the small pool of warm water. The minister baptized her in the name of Jesus and then carefully tipped her backwards and submerged her in the water. As soon as she was steady on her feet again, she climbed the steps on the opposite side. At the top, she turned to watch as Charlie's friend and some other men helped Charlie into the water. He too was baptized in the name of Jesus, and then submerged. With great care and strength, the men helped

Charlie up the opposite steps and out of the water. Together, he and Sandy went to the rest room to change back into their dry clothes.

It took all the strength that Charlie had to make the short trip to church to be baptized. But that day, he knew in his heart that he and Sandy were right with God.

> Peter replied, "Repent and be baptized, everyone of you, in the name of Jesus Christ for the forgiveness of your sins. And you will receive the gift of the Holy Spirit…" ACTS 2:38

Charlie came to realize that the words 'Everything will be alright' never did mean that he would beat the cancer and live a longer life with Sandy.

Charlie wrote a list of important details that would help Sandy in the future. He listed their financial assets and how to get to them. He made suggestions that would ease her transition into her new life without him.

During Charlie's last days, he continued to mull over the recent events. The vision of the man in his hospital room. The man's warm touch. His communication toward Charlie that everything would be alright. His purpose. The desire to be baptized. The baptisms.

Charlie, the man who protected his wife and his community, had come to understand that Jesus is Lord, and that He desires and deserves to be recognized publicly. Hence, the eleventh-hour baptisms.

Will the faith that Charlie and Sandy developed help their family and friends take a closer look at their own purpose on earth? Could that have been Charlie's purpose on earth, to encourage others to follow Jesus?

A week after the baptisms, Charlie died.

Sandy has no doubt in her mind that Charlie is resting in heaven now. She knows that the spiritual visitor that came to Charlie during that night, months before he died, was right: "Everything will be alright". And it is.

> … *Jesus replied, "The kingdom of God does not come with your careful observation, nor will people say, 'Here it is' or 'There it is,' because the kingdom of God is within you." LUKE 17:20*

He told me that I have a purpose in this life and if I did what he said, then everything would be alright.

Heaven Sent

by Gary & Peggy Shorter with Cheryl Mochau

Face it, God has His hands full! The world as we know it is big and heaven seems to be even bigger. After all, there are a lot of souls to host once they're done here on earth.

The Bible shows us that God is efficient and uses all of His creation to get His will done. Angels seem to be at the top of His list when it comes to getting messages sent in a timely fashion.

The angel Gabriel was sent to Zechariah to tell him that his elderly wife, Elizabeth, would soon bear a son and they were to name him John. Their child would grow up to be John The Baptist.

Six months after Elizabeth became pregnant, God sent Gabriel, the same angel, to tell her cousin Mary that she would soon conceive the Christ child.

> *"How will this be," Mary asked the angel, "since I am a virgin?" The angel answered, "The Holy Spirit will come upon you, and the power of the Most High will overshadow you. So the Holy One to be born will be called the Son of God. Even Elizabeth your relative is going to have a child in her old age, and she who was said to be barren is in her sixth month. For nothing is impossible with God."* LUKE 1:34

God sent an unnamed angel to tell Joseph that he should take Mary as his wife, even though she was with a child that was obviously not his own.

> *But after he had considered this* (divorcing Mary quietly), *an angel of The Lord appeared to him in a dream and said, "Joseph son of David, do not be afraid to take Mary home as your wife, because what is conceived in her is from the Holy Spirit. She will give birth to a son, and you are to give Him the name Jesus, because He will save His people from their sins."* MATTHEW 1:20

At the birth of the Christ child, first one angel, and then several more, appeared to inform the shepherds in a nearby field that Christ the Lord had been born in their town of Bethlehem.

> *Suddenly a great company of the heavenly host appeared with the angel, praising God and saying, "Glory to God in the highest, and on earth peace to men on whom His favor rests." When the angels had left them and gone into heaven, the shepherds said to one another, "Let's go to Bethlehem and see this thing that has happened, which the Lord has told us about."* LUKE 2:13

When Herod found out about the birth of the Christ child, he wanted to kill Him. An angel directed Joseph to take Mary and the baby Jesus to safety in Egypt. Scripture doesn't indicate the angel's name, but it does say that the same angel would later tell Joseph how long to stay in Egypt.

> *When they had gone, an angel of The Lord appeared to Joseph in a dream. He said, "Get up," he said, "take the child and his mother and escape to Egypt. Stay there until I tell you, for Herod is going to search for the child to kill Him."* MATTHEW 2:13

After Herod died, an angel of The Lord appeared in a dream to Joseph in Egypt and said, "Get up, take the child and his mother and go to the land of Israel, for those who were trying to take the child's life are dead." MATTHEW 2:19

The Bible tells us that angels are God's messengers, and that there is a hierarchy of angels, each with their own specific specialties.

For He will command His angels concerning you to guard you in all your ways; they will lift you up in their hands, so that you will not strike your foot against a stone. PSALM 91:11

However, not all angels have God's best interests in mind. Some have fallen from His grace.

And the angels who did not keep their positions of authority but abandoned their own home — these He has kept in darkness, bound with everlasting chains for judgment on the great Day. JUDE 1:6

For this reason, humans should not pray directly to angels, but should put their requests and thanks directly through to God, Jesus or The Holy Spirit, and let them direct the correct angels to fit the situation.

… It saves you by the resurrection of Jesus Christ, who has gone into heaven and is at God's right hand — with angels, authorities and powers in submission to Him. 1 PETER 3:21

Lest you be concerned that there are not enough angels to go around for all the needs in the world, take heart. When Jesus explained to His disciples that those who would cast off their evil ways and follow Him with the innocence of a child would be the greatest in heaven, He went on to say that each person on earth has an angel to watch over them. As those angels watch over us, they are always facing God. With that in mind, it isn't hard to imagine that they can alert Him for backup in an instant!

> Jesus said, *"See that you do not look down on one of these little ones. For I tell you that their angels in heaven always see the face of My Father in heaven."* MATTHEW 18:10

There have been many books written on the subject of angels helping people. In the book "The Case for Heaven; Near-Death Experiences as Evidence of the Afterlife" by Mally Cox-Chapman, the author has interviewed and documented several accounts of people who had encounters with celestial beings at the brink of their death. Many of the people interviewed have reported that something like an angel, or, in some cases, some kind of light-filled energy, had been sent to help many of the dying through the process. Some people report being given the option whether to stay on earth and endure the healing process or to go on toward the light with them.

My friends Gary and Peggy Shorter shared one such remarkable story of two brothers who had an angelic encounter in Vincennes, Indiana, in 1965.

There were two brothers, Junior and Mike, who were best friends. They loved to ride their motorcycle together. One sunny day they were out for a joyride. Junior was driving and Mike was riding on the back. There are no helmet laws in the state of Indiana, so neither young man was wearing one. Tragically, a car hit the motorcycle head-on. Junior, who was in front and driving, was thrown through the windshield of the on-coming car. His skull was cracked and his arms and legs broken. Mike's body was tossed over the car and he landed in a heap, leaving him with multiple injuries, including a badly cut wrist.

At the scene of the accident, an angel appeared to both young men and they had a conversation. The angel gave them a choice. He asked if they wanted to stay on earth, or go to heaven. Junior said he didn't have anything here that he wanted to live for, so he said he would like to go on to heaven. Mike told the angel that he had more living to do, so he wanted to stay on earth.

The broken bodies of the young men were taken by ambulance to St. Mary's Hospital, in Vincennes. Mike survived his injuries and is still alive and well at the time of this writing. His brother, Junior, went into a coma and died two weeks after the accident.

Mike has no doubt that angels exist, and has every assurance that Junior is in heaven.

The Bible tells us that angels are God's messengers, and that there is a hierarchy of angels, each with their own specific specialties.

How to Pray with Confidence

At first, the idea that we don't know how to pray may seem absurd to the faithful. Whether spoken out loud or silently, prayer is the language we use to connect with our creator. The Holy Spirit *is in us* and relays our prayers directly to God and Jesus. Only these three have the capability to know our unspoken thoughts.

Before we think *how to pray*, we need to ask ourselves, *why should we pray*? We pray because God, our Creator, is worthy of our prayers and rewards us according to His will and pleasure.

What is God's will? God has a divine plan for all people for the rest of time. Because He made us in His image, we are designed to be the working part of His will, also known as His plan. In the same way that a family pitches in together to get things done, so it is with the children of God. He has work for us to do, and when we're obedient, we do it. We're not perfect though, and He is aware of that.

What if we think we hear His command, but we don't follow through? Parents know the answer to this one right off. Parents love their children, no matter what. They experience joy or disappointment in their children's choices and actions. God experiences the same joy and disappointment in all of His children. And like any parent with multiple children, He does not hesitate to ask someone else to take care of a matter that another has failed to do. One way or another, God's will gets done!

God-given commands offer opportunities for individuals to grow in the Holy Spirit.

The Holy Spirit is a gift from God, given to each and every believer when they accept Jesus Christ, the Son of God, as their personal Savior. The Holy Spirit is *of* God and offers all believers wisdom and knowledge from heaven. This wisdom and knowledge does not just fall into people's laps. No, they must ask for it, and then open their minds to hear and understand it. The energy they put into gathering and using the knowledge is what hones and refines their faith, and develops their character.

Someone once described The Holy Spirit as a flowing ribbon of God's love, energy, wisdom and mercy that runs to and from God, in and out of each believer, adding and sifting our personal data, all the while looking out through our eyes with us. It's an awesome thought to me, the idea of a continuous ribbon filled with power from God, with no beginning and no end, that connects all believers to our Father God.

How do you pray? Do you get on your knees and run through your prayers quickly, so you can get off your knees? Do you sit in a favorite chair, with your Bible, note pad and a pen? Do you pray in bed as you go to sleep, or when you wake up? Do you whisper prayers all day long?

We won't know for sure until we get there, but something tells me that God loves to hear from us anytime, anywhere, any way. Like any parent, He loves it when His children call home.

A friend of mine has influenced my personal prayer time substantially. She said she always starts her prayers by asking

Jesus to forgive any sin that she might have committed since her last prayer time. She wants no blemish on her soul that would taint her and keep her from freely coming to God. She asks to be reminded of any sins she has done since she last spoke with God, which in her case, is every day. This done, she then feels free to move forward into her prayer time with confidence.

My friend stressed that she does not keep asking for forgiveness of past sins that have already been forgiven. To do so would be like telling Jesus that the sacrifice of His life just wasn't good enough to cover *her* sins, and that He needs to try again. Once we have asked for forgiveness of any sin, it is gone. Gone!

There is one sin that Jesus does not forgive. He called it the *eternal sin*, and it has to with the treatment of the Holy Spirit. The unforgivable sin is to be disrespectful, to lie about, or speak insultingly against the Holy Spirit or His ways. The Holy Spirit is the very essence of God, and Jesus does not take kindly to anyone speaking harshly against His Father.

> Jesus said, *"I tell you the truth, all the sins and blasphemies of men will be forgiven them. But whoever blasphemies against the Holy Spirit will never be forgiven; he is guilty of an eternal sin."* MARK 3:28

Does Mark 3:28 invoke fear that we must always be on guard with God, or face eternal retribution from Jesus? In a word, yes. The fear of God is a useful tool for developing a godly character that would only speak highly and lovingly of Him.

The chain reaction of disrespectful talk, insults or lies about the Holy Spirit may be overheard by unbelievers, and could stop them from ever seeking Jesus and attaining salvation. That is a stumbling block no Christian should be a part of.

What to do when life gets in the way of your relationship with God and prayer time is cut to a few minutes a day?

Jesus gave His disciples — and us — a model prayer:

> *He said to them, "When you pray, say: " 'Father, hallowed be Your Name, Your kingdom come. Give us each day our daily bread. Forgive us our sins, for we also forgive everyone who sins against us. And lead us not into temptation.' "* LUKE 11:2

Aside from reciting prayers written by others, how does one pray? There are no set rules, because prayer is a deeply personal thing. I tend to be conversational in my prayers, and I use notes. It's too easy to get off track and not cover all the issues in the time that is set aside for prayer. The notes keep me focused, and include many favorite Scripture verses, a listing of people and events to pray for, things I am thankful for, and world events. Daily issues, at home and around the world, keep my prayers fresh.

This is one of my favorite prayer outlines:

- Ask Jesus for forgiveness of any recent sins since we last spoke.
- Ask for guidance, wisdom and knowledge from the Holy Spirit.
- Pray for the growth of God's Kingdom, ministers, missionaries, all people.
- Pray for the leaders of our country, military, people in authority.
- Pray for my heart to seek God, increase my faith, stay close with prayer.
- Pray for God's will in my life and for those on the prayer list.
- Thank God for His spiritual blessings, His will in our lives.
- Pray blessings on the poor and the sick, the lost. List them by name.
- Pray to love others as Jesus does. To walk as Jesus walks.

- Pray for the courage to boldly tell others of Jesus' love.
- Thank Him for providing for our family and meeting every need.

Prayers are exercise for the soul. Prayers from the heart add strength and flexibility to the soul. They focus the light of love on one's faith walk, and straighten the path that leads to the narrow gate. Wisdom and knowledge from heaven funnel through the narrow gate along with the prayers on the lips of His beloved. The children of God need to be streaming through the narrow gate at all times!

> Jesus said, *"Enter through the narrow gate. For wide is the gate and broad is the road that leads to destruction, and many enter through it. But small is the gate and narrow the road that leads to life, and only a few find it."* MATTHEW 7:13

The Holy Spirit is of God and offers all believers wisdom and knowledge from heaven. This wisdom and knowledge does not just fall into people's laps. No, they must ask for it, and then open their minds to hear and understand it.

Beloved

Beloved. To me, it was always a squirmy word. A word that spoke of such intimacy that I was embarrassed to think of its depth. *Beloved.* Whispered in private between the closest of loved ones. Never to be shared lightly. Ministers tend to use the word to show their all-encompassing love for their congregations. The broadness of that seemed a little more tolerable, yet it still made me squirm. Was I taking the word too seriously? Had I somehow muddied the word with my own less-than-Puritanical background? I couldn't wrap my mind around the depth of the word.

October 21, 2006, was a perfect autumn day. Our young church was hosting its first seminar and we had sent invitations to all churches in our small city. A professor of theology at a seminary a couple of states away was invited to come, and we were committed to pay him handsomely to share his wisdom and knowledge of God with us.

The housekeeping team had buffed, polished and vacuumed every inch of the sanctuary and gathering area. My friends and I wanted to serve the freshest sandwiches possible, so we forfeited our time at the seminar and put together the most beautiful boxed lunches! We made them all quite fancy, adorning them with "Glory to God" stickers and matching ribbons. The lunches were fit for royalty!

At the 10:00 break, we greeted our guests with muffins, cookies, cans of soda and cups of hot coffee. Our guests embraced our hospitality with delight, and our faces beamed with joy that we could share our talents with so many.

After a quick cleanup, we rested before the lunch rush began. A few of the kitchen helpers slipped into the sanctuary to listen to the professor, but most of us just enjoyed visiting together and reveling in how smoothly things were going. We had a kitchen full of Marthas.

> *As Jesus and His disciples were on their way, He came to a village where a woman named Martha opened her home to Him. She had a sister called Mary, who sat at the Lord's feet listening to what He said. But Martha was distracted by all the preparations that had to be made.* LUKE 10:38

Lunchtime came and went. The food was eaten and we enjoyed the fellowship of serving side-by-side. We cleaned up the kitchen, and some went home. A few of us found empty seats in the back of the sanctuary, and listened to the remaining forty minutes of the seminar.

Beloved, blah, blah, blah. Oh no! There was that squirmy word that I always try my best to avoid. I must have missed all the good stuff while I was busy in the kitchen. Is that the kind of thanks I get for working through almost the entire seminar, only to come in for a few minutes at the end and have to hear how beloved everyone is? I eyed the door, but didn't dare try for it. After all, the speaker was supposed to be good. He came on high approval of the committee and getting up and walking out after I had just sat down, well, it seemed rude. Not very church-lady-like. So, I sat, and listened.

The professor caught my attention when he said, "Most

Christians know they are forgiven, but do they know they are God's *beloved*, as well?"

The professor continued speaking about being God's *beloved*. I relaxed and listened to the rhythm of his voice. Before long, a world rich with love opened up to me. "*Beloved*, you are God's own child and He loves you. He chose you to be His. He gave His Son so you, His *beloved* daughter, may have eternal life with Him in heaven. He knew you before you were born, and He looks forward to your coming home when He calls."

The professor went on to say that God knew none of us would be perfect. He knew we would sin, so He breathed love on us so we would get caught up on the wind of forgiveness, and forget trying to outrun Him in our shame. It's one thing to hear and learn this truth. It's another thing to accept it, to own it.

> *The fear of the Lord is the beginning of knowledge, but fools despise wisdom and discipline.* PROVERBS 1:7

It has been nineteen years since I surrendered and stopped trying to outrun God. Years before, He had sent some of His other converts after me, to bring me into the fold. They tried to love me as Jesus would, but I didn't yet know how to accept that kind of love. Finally, He sent one so close to His heart that there was no turning away.

At that time, Jesus was carefully explained and revealed to me. My doubt was replaced by truth and hope. Since that day, His Name has been etched on my soul. Father God was so pleased that He gave me the gift of His Spirit, which is still inside me, looking out through my eyes with me, connecting me to Him forever. One only does that for a *beloved*.

> *He who gets wisdom loves his own soul; he who cherishes understanding prospers.* PROVERBS 19:8

The professor concluded his talk with a quote from Deuteronomy

33:12: *"Let the beloved of the Lord rest secure in him, for He shields him all day long, and the one the Lord loves rests between His shoulders."* I wrote it down, pondered that statement and decided to claim it as a life verse.

The next morning, I woke up early and brought a cup of coffee into our family room. Opening my Bible, and placing it on my lap, it fell open to (where else but) Deuteronomy, chapter 33? My eyes fell right on verse 12, reinforcing that I am the Lord's *beloved*. He probably just wanted to be sure I heard Him the day before!

He has sent me little reminders ever since. One was on February 4, 2008, when I went on a job interview. An elderly couple wanted to stay in their own home, instead of going into an assisted living facility, so they decided to hire someone to come and cook healthy meals for them. That's what I do, so I went. To make a long story short, in the middle of the interview, the woman said she had something to share with me. In a foreign language she rattled off something and then smiled at me. I said that it sounded beautiful, and asked her what it meant. She said, "It means, 'You are my *beloved,* and I love you'."

Without missing a beat, I told her that after I got to know her a little bit better I would share with her what that meant to me. A few weeks later, I did just that. That's when she told me it was the only thing she knew how to say in Japanese, and that she didn't know why she felt compelled to say it to me!

The word *"beloved"* is no longer foreign to me, nor does it cause me to squirm. On the contrary, I kind of like to be called *"beloved"* now.

And I have *beloveds* of my own now too. Their Names roll off my lips like honey-butter. *Beloved* Father God. *Beloved* and forgiving Jesus. *Beloved* and closer-than-my-own-heart Holy Spirit. They are my *Beloveds,* and I love them. I know I am theirs. And so is every believer in Christ!

> *"Let the beloved of the Lord rest secure in him, for He shields him all day long, and the one the Lord loves rests between His shoulders."* DEUTERONOMY 33:12

The professor caught my attention when he said, "Most Christians know they are forgiven, but do they know they are God's beloved, as well?"

The Dove

It's been fifty years since Pat and Shirley got married. Together they have raised two boys and one girl, and have been blessed with six grandchildren, four boys and two girls. Pat and Shirley both worked hard to raise their children right and have many family stories full of humor and adventure, all shaped by the cornerstone of their Christian faith.

As a young couple in the 1950s, Pat and Shirley enjoyed the prosperity of life in Indiana. The United Sates was rebounding after the war and life in general was on the upswing. Hope was in the air. When Pat popped the question, Shirley was delighted to accept and get their lives moving forward together.

It was a typical hot and humid August day in 1959, when Pat picked Shirley up at her parents' home to go apply for their marriage license at City Hall. With the windows rolled down and the wind in their hair, they drove the winding country roads into town.

No sooner had they left Shirley's home, they noticed they were not alone. Flying an arm's length from Pat's open window was a gray dove. They saw it, watched it, commented *on* it, and *to* it. The bird flew alongside their car for several miles! As they approached the city limits, their bird escort flew off.

Pat and Shirley look back fondly on the dove that flew alongside them as they took steps to make a new life together. They believe it was a gift from God. Their marriage, though not always blissful, has always been blessed. They built their lives on the foundation of Jesus as Lord, God as the Father, and the Holy Spirit as the tie that binds them in love. The memory of the dove has been with them all through the years.

Then John gave this testimony: "I saw the Spirit come down from heaven as a dove and remain on Him..." JOHN 1:32

Hope was in the air. When Pat popped the question, Shirley was delighted to accept and get their lives moving forward together.

The Drummer

God blesses all of us with gifts and talents that are useful for the growth of His Kingdom. The musicians at our church are a prime example. They practice every Thursday evening for two or three hours, then come in an hour before the Saturday evening service, then again for the two Sunday morning services. The musicians at our church give much of their time for the growth of God's Kingdom. And they have a great time doing it!

> *Praise Him with the sounding of the trumpet, praise Him with the harp and lyre, praise Him with tambourine and dancing, praise Him with the strings and flute, praise Him with the clash of cymbals, praise Him with resounding cymbals.*
> PSALM 150:3

Our worship leader has a strong, sweet voice that fills all who hear it with melodic prayers. The backup singers compliment her lead with obvious grace and joy. The lead guitarist sings soulfully as he plays, all the while reflecting his love for God. The bass guitarist accompanies with his deep but tender baritone. On keyboard, the worship leader's daughter has been known to play and sing, sometimes while holding her own children on her lap. Her husband occasionally fills in for the bass guitarist and also plays the bongo drums.

The drummer is behind the clear plexiglass sound screen. His steady beat connects all the other instruments and voices. He is the glue that binds the sound of the band and gets the congregation clapping along. To meet the drummer in a setting away from church, one would never guess that he plays drums in a Christian rock band. His nature is gentle and humble, and when he speaks, it's with the soft voice of a thoughtful man.

The drummer has a lovely wife and a young daughter. The daughter enjoys being with her friends from Sunday school. His wife is always helping with something in one of the classrooms, in the sanctuary, or in the kitchen. Together, they stay late to sweep and lock up the church after services. This family gladly gives of themselves to our church. And except for the fact that the drummer's beat reverberates through the bones of everyone in the sanctuary, they do it quietly.

The drummer spends his days working at a local printing press company. A wonderful side effect of his time spent working with printed matter is that he has learned how to rescue and give new life to old, thin, torn paper.

One day my husband and he were talking. It came up that I had recently dropped my study Bible on the floor and it fell apart. The drummer asked how bad the damage was, and my husband told him the book had separated into a few pieces at the binding, but the worst was that a couple of pages had torn through the text, in the middle of the book, right at the binding. The drummer seemed to light up a little at this news. He offered to try to fix it.

The next week I handed him the pieces of my Bible in a paper bag and assured him that if it were not possible to fix it, I would be okay with it. I had been thinking of getting another one and transferring my notes over into it. Calmly, he took my Bible and said he would do his best, and then laid it on the seat where he and his family would sit during the sermon.

One week later, the drummer approached me with a smile on his face. He handed me the Bible, and it was as good as new! I couldn't believe he was able to put it all back together. Then he showed me the pages where it had torn at the binding. He had managed to piece the text back together so it was legible from both sides of the page. I couldn't believe what he had done with those thin, torn pages!

> *Who is wise and understanding among you? Let him show it by his good life, by deeds done in the humility that comes from wisdom.* JAMES 3:13

Now heaven help the drummer who helped me with my broken Bible! I am not one to keep this kind of secret quiet for long. My friends have been lining up to have him fix their Bibles too. Graciously, he fixes them. Quietly he helps grow the Kingdom of God!

God loves and honors those who give of themselves for the glory of His Kingdom. The drummer's family is blessed by God, and in turn they bless God's people in a quiet, unassuming manner. And in the same way, the church band offers up musical prayers that glorify God and help the congregation worship Him in a delightful way. The beat goes on!

> *Praise the Lord. How good it is to sing praises to our God, how pleasant and fitting to praise Him!* PSALM 147:1

This family gladly gives of themselves to our church. And except for the fact that the drummer's beat reverberates through the bones of everyone in the sanctuary, they do it quietly.

The Group Home Friends

Making the choice to send a mentally challenged child away to live in a group home does not come easy to most families. Most will change their own lives drastically to keep their child at home for as long as possible. However, eventually for some the disruption to the rest of the family and the child's need for constant supervision wins out. The search starts for the best- and nearest- facility to place their loved one.

There are group homes for mentally challenged children and adults in residential neighborhoods all over the country. The residents are given the opportunity to live and thrive in a family setting. They go to school, work, and come home afterward to help with light chores and do homework just like families everywhere.

Most group home staffs are carefully screened and chosen for their integrity and ability to love others. Those are the things most families are looking for when they reach the point of placing their child in such a facility. But how does one measure love when reading a brochure or meeting with the admissions personnel?

We are therefore Christ's ambassadors, as though God were making His appeal through us. 2 CORINTHIANS 5:20

Sue worked in a group home for girls, ages nine- to twenty-one, while she attended college. Upon graduation, she came on full-time, bringing her knowledge of early childhood studies with her. It was a decision of the heart to stay on at the group home. Sue's degree would enable her to earn more money elsewhere, but during the past four years, she had come to know and love the girls in this group home. At the time, Sue thought it best to stay put until a teaching job opened up for her.

> *Remember this: Whoever sows sparingly will also reap sparingly, and whoever sows generously will also reap generously.* 2 CORINTHIANS 9:6

Sue was "best friends" with Amy, one of the higher functioning residents. When Sue was in the house, they were inseparable. Sue had been disciplined by her superiors to be very careful with favoritism. Amy showed signs of jealousy when Sue interacted with the other girls and that wasn't good for any of them. Sue decided to turn the energy of Amy's jealousy into love for others and it became a life lesson for all who looked on.

A new girl had just been sent to live at the group home. She was nine years old, had never been away from her family, spoke about ten questionable words, and she was wild. No one could get near her on her first day at the home. For their own protection, the other girls were separated from her. She was assigned to Sue.

After supper was cleaned up, the girls all bathed, got into their pajamas, and settled down in front of the television in the family room. It was a Saturday night, and "Soul Train" was on. While it may not have been the most calming of shows to watch just before bedtime, everyone loved "Soul Train"!

Sue was in the next room with the new girl, Mandy. It was a bedroom with a half-door. The top section was removed, and the bottom half could be locked. It was a safe, visible place for time out. Mandy had been thrashing out at Sue when she suddenly heard the "Soul Train" music. Immediately, Mandy tried to climb over the door so she could watch it with the other girls. Sue held her back, knowing she was still violent and could hurt one of the others without warning. There was a scuffling and two other staff members came to the door to offer help. Sue waved them off.

As the music on the television switched over to a commercial, Sue managed to get a hold of Mandy and hug her close. She wrapped both arms around Mandy and started rocking her and talking softly, soothing her with loving words. Mandy responded instantly! She went from wild child to sweet child in a matter of seconds. She smiled broadly and snuggled into Sue's shoulder as Sue hugged her closely. Then the "Soul Train" music started up again. Mandy squirmed to get out of Sue's arms, but she held her tight. Sue asked Mandy if she wanted to watch it from the door, so they did. They stood together, leaning over the door looking into the family room. They even danced to the music together. The other staff did not interfere. This was Sue at her best.

Amy, on the other hand, was gearing up for a jealous tantrum. Sue saw it brewing. During the next commercial, she called to Amy and asked if she would like to come in and meet Mandy after the show was over. Amy was visibly glad for the attention and she agreed.

Amy's brooding tension disappeared after she walked into the bedroom right into a group hug. The three of them sat quietly and talked about how much fun they could all have in the group home once Mandy got used to everything. Sue asked Amy to help Mandy get over being homesick. It was a happy time for all three of them. They were the Three Musketeers!

The wise in heart are called discerning, and pleasant words promote instruction. PROVERBS 16:21

During the next two years, Mandy thrived. Her vocabulary grew from ten words to two hundred. She gained control of her anger at being separated from her family. She started drawing and sending them pictures and using the telephone to call home on certain evenings. She developed cooking skills and looked forward to coming home from school to help with supper. Mandy was the youngest girl in the group home and was rapidly becoming the highest functioning.

Mandy's parents visited her every two weeks and were overjoyed with her progress. They had been overwhelmed having her at home. She was unpredictable, and more often than not, violent, with their other child. Although it was heart-wrenching at the time, choosing to place Mandy in the group home turned out to be a good decision for their whole family.

Amy's family noticed a growing maturity in her, as well. They also visited their daughter every couple of weeks, and were delighted with her new desire to help others. There was always that underlying jealousy, but she managed to control it. She showed a remarkable sense of duty and love to the other girls, especially to Mandy.

It takes a special type of person to work with mentally challenged people. Knowledge and skills are fine, but it's the added element of love that makes it all come together. Sue had it all together.

> *How much better to get wisdom than gold, to choose understanding rather than silver!* PROVERBS 16:16

Sue decided to turn the energy of Amy's jealousy into love for others and it became a life lesson for all who looked on.

The Group Home Warmth

Wilma came to the group home as a child care worker on the first day the leaves started to change from green to reds and yellows, in 1983. She was a middle-aged woman, a recent immigrant from Poland, and she brought with her a love for nature. Upon meeting the girls, she delighted in telling everyone, in detail, how the trees grew and why their leaves changed colors. Her accent was thick, and it was hard to keep up with her as she spoke. She was full of life, and we hung on her every word.

Wilma loved living in America, but her whole family still lived in Poland. Her heartstrings and her purse strings were stretched across the ocean. Aside from her forty-hours-a-week at the group home, Wilma supplemented her income as a massage therapist. She had a table that folded up neatly and a bag of assorted oils and lotions that she liked to use in her trade. She kept those items in her car just in case she needed them at a moment's notice.

The laborer's appetite works for him; his hunger drives him on. PROVERBS 16:26

This is a story about Wilma and a resident at the group home. Let's call her Lisa. Lisa was about sixteen years old, but was as small as an eight year old. No one could be thinner and still walk. She moved so slowly that it was painful to watch. Not that she was in pain, or any that we were aware of, she just didn't have the energy to put one foot in front of the other. Her mind seemed to move just as slowly as her body. Ask Lisa a question, and it took upwards of twenty seconds to get her to make eye contact. She heard, and when given time, she reacted. She was a sweet girl, but her constant runny nose was a bit of a turn off. It's hard to hug someone when they have a runny nose. If she even realized it, Lisa just didn't have the energy to wipe it away or to try to sniff it back up.

Wilma took an instant liking to Lisa. On Wilma's first evening, after supper, when the girls were all sitting on the couches in the family room watching television, she sat next to Lisa. Wilma held Lisa's little blue hand in hers and remarked on how cold she felt. The massage therapist in her took over and she lightly rubbed Lisa's hands and wrists with her strong hands as they watched television. Normal flesh color came into her fingers and hands within a couple of minutes. Lisa smiled at Wilma and a bond was formed.

> *Be joyful in hope, patient in affliction, faithful in prayer. Share with God's people who are in need. Practice hospitality.*
> ROMANS 12:12

Each evening after that, Wilma and Lisa would sit together. Wilma was intrigued with the rapid color changes in Lisa's hands and started to massage her feet as well. It seems that massaging Lisa's feet was the magic bullet. The girl changed. She started moving a little faster when she got up to go to bed. As weeks went by, she progressively altered her usual slow shuffle into full strides when she walked. She was far more alert than she had ever been. Everyone was commenting on Lisa's new energy!

It doesn't take a massage therapist to rub some love into cold, dry souls. Wilma used her gift from God to transfer the warmth of her own hands into those of one less fortunate.

… But each man has his own gift from God; one has this gift, another has that. 1 CORINTHIANS 7:7

The girl changed. She started moving a little faster when she got up to go to bed. As weeks went by, she progressively altered her usual slow shuffle into full strides when she walked.

The Ladder

It's been said that God is in the details. He sees what we are doing and straightens our path. He sends a friend, or a future spouse, or even a ladder if that's what we need.

My husband and I had been living in our home for a few years when he lost his job in an economic downturn. We had accumulated a nice stash of savings, but were worried about running through it too quickly for incidentals. It was supposed to be for our retirement, after all. Other than that, we planned to use it for emergencies, but it was not meant to live on.

In Matthew 6:31, Jesus explained that by putting faith in the one who created us, we would have everything needed to live. *"So do not worry, saying, 'What shall we eat?' or 'What shall we drink?' or 'What shall we wear?' For the pagans run after all these things, and your heavenly Father knows that you need them…"*

Our home was showing typical signs of aging and we needed a ladder to make a few simple repairs. I drove out to one of the big-box stores to price them, only to leave empty-handed. The one ladder we would need was upwards of two hundred dollars. I couldn't bring myself to spend that kind of money on something we would use rarely.

On the short drive home, I laid out the problem to God and told Him about our dilemma. Wouldn't you know, a few blocks from our street was a yard sale, and, well, you can guess what happened. There were two ladders to choose from. I bought the twenty dollar extension ladder and someone helped me load it into the car.

> *Trust in the Lord with all your heart and lean not on your own understanding; in all your ways acknowledge Him, and He will make your path straight.* PROVERBS 3:5

Once at home, my husband came out to see why I was parked so oddly in the driveway. He was delighted to see our "new" ladder. Now, seven years later, that ladder leans in its own place in our garage and is ready whenever we are.

Some folks might say that was a coincidence. The yard sale was there when I went to the store and so was the ladder. True, but it was a little out of my way and I was focused on getting a new ladder. I asked God for help and He efficiently directed me to the yard sale with two perfectly functional ladders at a price I was delighted to pay. There was even a young man at the sale who was happy to lift the ladder into the car for me. No, that was not a coincidence.

> *"Ask and it will be given to you; seek and you shall find; knock and the door will be opened for you. For everyone who asks receives; he who seeks finds; and to him who knocks, the door will be opened."* MATTHEW 7:7

No, that was not a coincidence.

Moe's Famous Dressing

by Cindy (Moe) McClanahan

Every year, for 25 years, I have been blessed to cook Christmas dinner for the whole family: parents, brothers, sisters, in-laws, nieces, nephews, grandchildren and great-grandchildren. Living in a small town most of my life, everyone knew everyone else. I was extremely close to my church family, so it was only fitting that anyone with nowhere else to enjoy Christmas dinner was invited to our house. The total was usually around 40 or 45 people.

> *Taste and see that the Lord is good; blessed is the man who takes refuge in Him.* PSALM 34:8

I, being the Martha Stewart type, made sure I did it all. Of course, there was roasted turkey, and my specialty, the one thing everyone raved about, *Moe's Famous Dressing*. There were plenty of mashed potatoes, gravy, green beans, corn, cranberry relish, home-made bread, and pumpkin and pecan pies. Most of the time, after two solid days of cooking, it turned out pretty darn good. Well, that was until the year of 1985.

I was going about my business making sure everything on the menu was coming along on schedule. As usual, I made the dressing a day in advance, so it could soak up all the wonderful flavors I was so proud of. On Christmas morning, I tasted it before it went in the oven to make sure it was good. "WHAT?!? FLAT?" I said out loud to know one in particular. So I put another tablespoon of sage in (so I thought), but still no taste. So I put another tablespoon of sage in (so I thought)… still no taste. Thinking that maybe it was a little old, I put another big dash of sage in (so I thought). By now, this was at least a quarter-cup of sage. Any good cook knows that would be entirely too much sage. Then it dawned on me to look at the label again.

I let out a bloodcurdling cry. "OH NO! It was CUMIN!" My husband and children, who were still very young at the time, all came running. I explained what I had done, and, of course, began to cry. Cumin, native to the eastern Mediterranean, is a very spicy aromatic herb used in many southwestern dishes. Cumin is *not* intended for Moe's Famous Dressing!

Right there in the kitchen I fell to my knees begging Jesus to intervene. "Make it right, Lord" I prayed aloud. "I know you can fix it." I continued to pray while everyone said to just let it go. Being kind, they assured me that we really didn't need dressing for the Christmas meal.

> *In my distress I called to the Lord; I called out to my God.*
> *From His temple He heard my voice; my cry came to His ears.*
> 2 SAMUEL 22:7

Listening to that small, still, inner voice, I decided to let go and let God take over. I baked the oddly-seasoned dressing. As my company arrived, I said nothing about it. It wasn't long before we all sat down to eat. I held my breath while I watched each person taste *Moe's Famous Dressing*. It was unanimous: it was the best dressing ever! With a long sigh, I let the story unfold. No one could believe what had happened. To my surprise most of them suggested I do it just the same way again next year!

... The man with two tunics should share with him who has none, and the one who has food should do the same. LUKE 3:11

I knew my precious Savior was in on it. He knew how special it was for me to feed so many people I cared about on Christmas day. He knew how special it was to share my gifts and talents with so many people who had nowhere else to eat on this special day. He was in control the whole time.

I never used cumin again.

I did learn some very valuable lessons that day. God hears every prayer, large and small, but He won't hear our requests if we don't ask! God knows His way around the kitchen and excels at spicing things up. And finally, even as good as we always believed it to be, *Moe's Famous Dressing* is nothing without the special gift of the Lord's touch!

---

*I did learn some very valuable lessons that day —
God hears every prayer, large and small, but He won't
hear our requests if we don't ask! God knows His way
around the kitchen and excels at spicing things up.*

Midwest Comfort

My work as a Personal Chef connects me with all kinds of people. Most people would really like to have a Personal Chef, but only a very small segment of the population can afford the costly luxury. I specialize in healthy diets, making it my mission to bring wholesome, healthy food to people's tables.

Over the years, my clients have come and gone for various reasons. Whenever I have needed another cooking client, it seemed that all I had to do was ask God to send me one, and He would. Since these are matches made in heaven, I have become very good friends with most of my clients through the years.

The odd thing is, as much as I talk freely with God every day, asking Him for help is not always the first thing that comes to mind. Generally, I would ask other clients if they knew anyone, or I would occasionally advertise in hopes of finding someone new. But it seems that the minute I brought my request to Him with sincerity and faithful expectation, then someone would call looking for help with a food dilemma. After a short phone interview, we would schedule a meeting to discuss in-depth needs. Nine times out of ten, they would become a new client.

> *Commit to the Lord whatever you do, and your plans will succeed.* PROVERBS 16:3

Soon after moving to the Midwest, I started cooking for a young couple with a five-year-old girl. The first day I arrived at their home to cook, they had left for work and school, so I let myself in with the key. To my delight, there was a welcoming note for me on the kitchen table from the three of them. They expressed their gratitude and told me how much they were looking forward to coming home that evening to have dinner together. I cherish notes like that.

This kitchen had all the right appliances and more! Nestled between the sink and the big stove was a well-used, pint-sized, pink kitchen stove and oven set. There were tiny pans with lids, assorted cookie cutters, pot holders, and pink dishes, too.

As I looked around the kitchen at the wallpaper border that had prayers to God printed on it, and saw the little girl's art that decorated the refrigerator door, I knew this was a loving home. The essence of this family's love hung in the air even hours after they had left.

To this day, few things sing to my heart quite the way that little kitchen set did the first time I saw it.

When families cook and eat together, it gives them time to unwind. It's a precious time to share and care about each other's lives. God loves that!

> *By wisdom a house is built, and through understanding it is established; through knowledge its rooms are filled with rare and beautiful treasures.* PROVERBS 24:3

Whenever I have needed another cooking client, it seemed that all I had to do was ask God to send me one, and He would.

The HOLY LORD House

One day as I was happily cooking meals for a client in her kitchen, the door bell rang. A frail old man stood there. Slowly, he introduced himself as the retired rabbi next door. He had locked himself out of his house and came to get the key that he had given the homeowner several years earlier. I showed him a small rack of keys near the kitchen door, but he did not recognize any as his. I called the homeowner at work and she vaguely remembered trading keys with him, but said if it wasn't on that rack, then she had no clue where it was. I gave him the bad news, and he graciously accepted it. He looked thirsty so I handed him a bottle of cold water, which he thanked me for. Turning, he called back that he would wait on his patio behind the house until his wife got home from the grocery store. He was sure she would not be long.

I went back to work and peeked out the window from time-to-time to check on him. He seemed totally fine. It was a beautiful back yard, as they all were on that street. The Atlantic Ocean was just a block away. The sounds of sea gulls and ship horn blasts were commonplace. The scent of the ocean blew in on the breeze most of the time.

About an hour later, I finished my work and headed out to my car to put away my tools. I brought him another bottle of water and a few cookies fresh from the oven. He was glad to have them and offered me a seat. He apologized for being so much trouble and I assured him he wasn't any trouble at all. I apologized for not being able to produce a house key for him and he agreed that that would have been nice. We enjoyed each other's company and he shared a story about his house.

"Have you ever been inside my home?" he asked. I assured him that I had not.

He went on to say "We call our home The HOLY LORD House."

Coming from a very old retired rabbi, I was totally intrigued. "Why is that?" I asked.

He told me that the Pilgrims first built a modest structure on this spot back in the 1600s. Over the years, his home had been built up and over the original structure, mostly as a way to preserve it, but also for economical reasons. He told me that the ceiling beams in his home were hand-hewn from large rustic logs. What makes them even more special is that they have "HOLY LORD", followed by Scripture, carved all over them!

I found delight that this retired rabbi had made his home on the same ground, using some of the same hand-carved timbers, that Christians had chosen more than four hundred years before.

> Jesus said in John 10:14, "… *I know my sheep and my sheep know me — just as the Father knows me and I know the Father — and I lay down my life for the sheep. I have other sheep that are not of this sheep pen. I must bring them also…*"

He invited me to come visit him at home some other time. Sadly, I moved away from the area before I had the opportunity to see the inside of his HOLY LORD House. I would have liked to have seen it with my own eyes, but just hearing about it has left a lasting impression.

Years went by, several clients came and went, and one day a client in Indiana informed me that a painter would be at her house the following week to do some work. It seems she was having the wall between the kitchen and the family room painted with a mural of the Fruit of the Spirit scripture. Her friend Terri, a professional painter, offered to paint it as a housewarming gift. Now these beautiful words are hand-painted in a lovely script: *Galatians 5:22 The Fruit of the Spirit is love, joy, peace, patience, kindness, goodness, faithfulness, gentleness and self-control.*

I never did get to see the inside of the HOLY LORD house, but I have been blessed to work in the FRUIT OF THE SPIRIT house!

> *So I (Paul) say, live by the Spirit, and you will not gratify the desires of the sinful nature.* GALATIANS 5:16

I found delight that this retired rabbi had made his home on the same ground, using some of the same hand carved timbers, that Christians had chosen more than four hundred years before.

Holy Health Food!

It wasn't long after God created the heavens and the earth that He eventually made humans. Being forward thinking, He designed and developed their power source in the form of plants, animals and fish. Like any good host has done since, God figured out the menu before inviting His guests over. He thought about what they would like, dislike, were allergic to, or just shouldn't have, and took care to have everything on hand for them to eat. He paid attention to the needs of every cell in their bodies.

> *Then God said, "I give you every seed bearing plant on the face of the whole earth and every tree that has fruit with seed in it. They will be yours for food."* GENESIS 1:29

That piece of scripture makes it obvious that God meant for us to be vegetarians at first. But after the flood, when Noah and his family had successfully completed the mission of getting pairs of all creatures to safety, God expanded the menu.

> *Then God blessed Noah and his sons, saying to them, "Be fruitful and increase in number and fill the earth. The fear and dread of you will fall upon all the beasts of the earth, and all the birds of the air, upon every creature that moves along the ground, and upon all the fish of the sea; they are given into your hands. Everything that lives and moves will be food for you. Just as I gave you the green plants, now I give you everything."* GENESIS 9:1

Being a chef, I'm finding it difficult to write a book that doesn't contain recipes. The following few recipes are jam-packed with many of the vitamins and nutrients that are necessary to run our bodies efficiently. When prepared correctly, they may be considered to be healing foods, as well.

Antioxidants occur naturally in whole foods and are designed to track down and consume cancer-causing free radicals in the body, leaving them inactive and unable to cause disease and premature aging. It's important to prepare all foods carefully to maintain the integrity of their health-giving benefits.

High heat is probably the fastest way to damage or destroy delicate nutrients in foods. Deep-fat fried foods get crispy when cooked in hot oil. Unfortunately, high temperatures break down the quality of the oil, which then penetrates and damages the food.

Grilled food gets its flavor from a little char and the smoke that flares up from the fat that drips onto the hot coals. Studies show that smoked foods are carcinogenic, and too much char isn't so good for the body either.

Even sautéing foods in hot oil on top of the stove can have dangerous results. Have you ever burned oil in a skillet and noticed how it turns dark, smokes and forms coagulated oil slicks? Left alone, hot oil will eventually burst into flames. Burnt oil, and any particles it forms, needs to be wiped out and discarded. Damaged oil that is consumed by the human body may damage the tender cells that make up the walls of veins, arteries, and organs, as it bumps and drags its way out of the body.

By now, you must be wondering how to prepare food in a good and wholesome manner. For starters, when cooking on the stovetop, use medium- to low-heat. Unless you're bringing water to a boil, don't blast the heat in an effort to get it to cook everything fast. Start with a lower temperature and let it climb gradually. Instead of using vegetable cooking spray, butter or oil in a skillet, try using fat-free chicken broth or water to keep foods from sticking. The absence of oil will give the food a cleaner taste and provide fewer calories. The trace of fat in the broth will help sautéed foods to brown lightly.

The first recipe calls for fresh asparagus spears. Thick asparagus spears should be peeled before using. For best results, use a vegetable peeler for that job. If the spears are thin, it is not necessary to peel them. Start by trimming about three inches off the bottom of the stalk and discard it. To clean any sand or dirt from the layered tips, simply place the tops of the asparagus stalks upside down in a small bowl or cup of cold water and let them soak for a few minutes. Before using, shake the tips vigorously to remove excess water, along with any particles of trapped sand or dirt.

Roasted Asparagus Parmesan   serves 4

1 tablespoon canola oil
1 pound thin asparagus spears, trimmed, cleaned
1 teaspoon Mrs. Dash Garlic
1 tablespoon grated parmesan cheese

Preheat the oven to 375 degrees. Pour the oil onto a large baking sheet with sides (a jelly roll pan is perfect), set aside. Place the trimmed tops on the prepared baking sheet, sprinkle with the seasoning and cheese. Bake for 12-15 minutes, or until fork tender.

Salmon is a good source of Omega-3 oil, which is necessary for building strong, resilient cell membranes. The white wine adds a flash of taste, but chicken broth or plain water may be substituted if you wish. I use mild prepared horseradish and find it combines well with honey to give the Orange-Horseradish Sauce a nice blend of sweet and heat.

Salmon with Orange-Horseradish Sauce   serves 4

12 ounces fresh salmon fillet, skin removed
1 tablespoon lemon juice
1 tablespoon dry white wine
1 teaspoon Mrs. Dash Original
1/2 cup plain yogurt
1 tablespoon prepared horseradish
1 tablespoon honey
1/2 cup drained mandarin oranges
1/2 teaspoon parsley flakes

Preheat the oven to 375°. Lightly coat a baking sheet with vegetable cooking spray. Place the fish on the baking sheet, and sprinkle with the lemon juice, wine and seasoning. Bake for 12-15 minutes or until done. Meanwhile, make the sauce in a small bowl by using the remaining ingredients. When the fish is done cooking, top with the sauce.

Try this inexpensive, yet highly nutritious soup recipe. If kale has too strong a flavor for your family, substitute spinach instead.

Kale Pepper Pot Soup   serves 4

1 cup water or broth
1/2 sweet red bell pepper, chopped
1/2 yellow bell pepper, chopped
1/2 green bell pepper
1 cup onion, chopped
1 tablespoon minced garlic
1 cup sweet potato, peeled, minced
15 ounces canned pinto beans, drained
1 cup diced tomatoes, with juice
4 cups fat-free chicken broth
1 cup water
1/2 cup uncooked pasta (orzo or elbows)
2 cups kale or spinach, chopped

1 tablespoon salt free seasoning

Heat the liquid in a large pot, add the peppers, onion, garlic and sweet potato. Cook over medium-high heat until tender and most of the water evaporates, about six or seven minutes. Add the beans, tomatoes, broth and water, cover, bring back to a boil. Add the pasta, reduce the heat to simmer for 10 minutes. Stir in the kale and seasoning, cook for about one minute, or until the kale turns a darker shade of green. Remove from the heat. Serve hot.

The No-Bake Fruit Cake was developed in my kitchen one hot July afternoon for my sister's birthday celebration. She was on a diet to lose weight and asked me not to make a fattening birthday cake that would thwart her plans. This cake was the result. For best results, select the largest elongated watermelon you can find.

No-Bake Fruit Cake   serves 12 or more

1 cup blueberries, rinsed and drained
1 cup strawberries, rinsed and drained
1 cup mandarin oranges, drained
1 kiwi fruit, peeled and sliced
12 cherries with stems
16 ounces custard style vanilla yogurt
1 whole large seedless watermelon

Wash, and let the fruit dry on paper toweling. Slice the strawberries and kiwi thin. Leaving the watermelon flesh in one piece, remove the rind. Cut a flat "bottom" from the thickest end so it stands upright. Trim the flesh in three thick, graduated layers, the bottom one being largest and the top being the smallest. Starting at the top, spoon the yogurt down the sides of the melon in a cascading fashion. Spread the fruit decoratively on the extended surfaces and top with the cherries, stems standing straight up. Cut as you would any extremely tall cake and serve on long narrow plates.

These recipes include only a few of the highly nutritious foods that God created to fuel our bodies. He has given us such a wide variety of foods to use that it's easy to imagine Him wanting us to enjoy them.

To keep food from becoming boring, feel free to interchange other similar foods for those listed here. Be mindful to use your heat sources with care to prevent damaging the nutrient value of the foods. And always, always, give thanks to God for providing all of your needs, especially for the abundance of delicious food He designed for us to use!

> *"… He has shown kindness by giving you rain from heaven and crops in their seasons; he provides you with plenty of food and fills your hearts with joy."* ACTS 14:17

He paid attention to the needs of every cell in their bodies.

What to Do
When You've Blown It

It was a hot Saturday evening, in June of 2005, when Pastor Glenn Howell delivered the first of three sermons for the weekend. The title was "What to Do When You've Blown It". The media screen displayed a large open book with lists of fictitious names. It was called the Book of Life. As the pages full of names turned, he talked about the weight of sin on individuals and on the world at large.

Pastor Glenn talked about all kinds of sins, including lies, cheating, divorce and murder. He left no stone unturned. Just so you don't get the wrong idea, Pastor Glenn is not a fire and brimstone sort of guy. He's more of a soft peddler who carries a velvet hammer.

Blushed cheeks and downcast eyes showed that Pastor Glenn had hit nerves throughout the congregation. To his credit, he didn't leave us all with a feeling of doom and gloom for more than a few moments.

He was saying that those who knew Jesus as their Savior already knew what a relief it was to have the burdens of sins lifted. They knew the feeling of relief that comes from no longer carrying the weight of negativity on their minds. He reminded the faithful that the Holy Spirit knows every heart and prompts each person to seek forgiveness from Jesus for sins.

Pastor Glenn reminded the congregation that Jesus wants everyone to recover from all sins. He wants believers to come to Him so they may enjoy a lifetime of clean living and loving in the family of God. Counting out on his fingers, Pastor Glenn pointed out how anyone can make that happen:

- Ask Jesus for forgiveness and a change of heart.
- Identify and turn away from sinful actions.
- Accept responsibility for our sins, take the punishment and move on.

Pastor Glenn reminded us that there is no end to the trouble sin can cause, so recognize sin, and stop doing it. Apologize to Jesus for the sin, then go to whoever was hurt by it and apologize to them. Promise not to do it again. The old fashioned word for it is *repent*. Repent means to see the problem, stop it in its tracks and change the behavior so it doesn't have a chance to happen again.

Once the sin has been tagged, do a one-eighty and don't look back. This may require a change in friends, a new place to hang out and a new train of thought. Familiar grooves in the old path may help you feel secure, or even happy for awhile, but eventually they will drag you down deeper and will trip you up again. He reminded everyone that the best way to get out of the rut of sinning is to disassociate yourself with that old path and those old friends.

Go for change in a big way. Make a new, fresh path and boldly ask Jesus and the Holy Spirit for direction. They like it when their family walks in boldness!

> *When I called, you answered me; you made me bold and stouthearted.* PSALM 138:3

Learn to keep Jesus' name on the tip of your tongue, and call out to Him for all things, whether big or small. He will lead you. He will be right there to help you do the right thing. With Jesus, no job is too big, no job is too small.

> *Be joyful always; pray continually; give thanks in all circumstances, for this is God's will for you in Christ Jesus.* 1 THESSALONIANS 5:16

In closing, it cannot be repeated too many times: Jesus is the Son of God. Jesus and the Holy Spirit keep the communication flowing between humans and God. Jesus takes away our sins, but only if we ask Him to. The Holy Spirit lives right inside us, and there is no fooling one so close. He knows our motives. Both Jesus and the Holy Spirit help us to clean up and live pure lives so we may approach our Father God with confidence and love, and to be clean and holy when we do.

Pastor Glenn's advice for a blessed life:

- Recognize your sins.
- Admit them to Jesus.
- Ask for forgiveness.
- Spend time alone with God every day, ten minutes or an hour.
- Ask God for a change of heart, guidance to know how to live right.
- Ask Jesus to show you a change of direction in your life.
- Don't follow the crowd; be selective, go through the narrow gate.
- Ask the Holy Spirit for knowledge and wisdom to build a good life.
- Ask God, Jesus and the Holy Spirit for a life filled with love and joy.
- Share your God moments so others desire and seek love, joy and peace.

... Forgetting what is behind and straining toward what is ahead, I press on toward the goal to win the prize for which God has called me heavenward in Christ Jesus. PHILIPPIANS 3:13

Go for change in a big way. Make a new, fresh path and boldly ask Jesus and the Holy Spirit for direction.

About The Writers

Vicki Brasel owns a State Farm Agency in Evansville, Indiana, where her dog, Muffi, is the official office greeter. Vicki dedicates much of her life to mentoring women and girls at Evansville's Grace House — Teen Challenge and at the Dream Center. She frequently serves on teams for Chrysalis and Journey weekends. Vicki's favorite relationship of all time is the one she has with Jesus Christ.

Marlina Easton has helped many people come to know Jesus Christ as their Lord and Savior through her bold and revealing lifestyle and discussions about Him. She is retired from the restaurant industry, and lives in Connecticut with her husband, James.

Cheryl Brown Folz is a wife, mother and civil engineer. Cheryl has been involved with youth ministries for years. She lives in Southwest Indiana with her husband, Jeff, and their two daughters.

Robin Lannert is delighted to be called a "daughter of God". Robin lives in Southwest Indiana with her husband Dennis. They have two sons, Nick and Cory. Robin uses her expertise as a dental hygienist to nurture and care for a multitude of children, including those in the country of Myanmar, in Southeast Asia.

Cindy McClanahan lives in Southwestern Indiana with her husband of 35 years, Randal. They have three grown children and four grandchildren. Cindy is owner and operator of *Cindy's Interline Cruises*, specializing in selling cruises to airline employees and the U.S. military.

Cheryl Mochau is a personal chef, writer and speaker. She is the owner and operator of *Cheryl Really Cooks! Personal Chef Service*, author of the cookbook *A Personal Chef Cooks: Recipes From a Decade of Lower Fat Cooking*, and writes for various magazines. Cheryl lives in Southwestern Indiana with her husband, Geoff.

Christa Shore, a native of Indiana, is a minister, singer/songwriter, and visual artist. Christa Shore began sharing her music as a worship leader in local churches during the '90s. In 2001 her band *Beyond the Veil* was established and has since recorded two albums: *Beauty from Ashes* and *Dance Before It's Done*. Christa leads conferences and concerts across the United States, as well as weekend *Beyond the Veil Fellowship* worship services in Evansville, Indiana, with her husband, Mike. They have two adult children: son Curt and daughter Shari.

Gary Shorter, born in Carlisle, Indiana, currently lives in Mount Vernon, Indiana, with Peggy, his wife of 46 years. Gary is an artist who enjoys painting and recording Gospel and Country Western music. Gary is a United States Marine Corps veteran.

Peggy Shorter, of Hammond, Indiana, lives with her husband, Gary, in Mount Vernon, Indiana. Peggy is a homemaker who enjoys trying out new recipes, gardening, decorating and entertaining family and friends in her home.

Phil Young is a retired chimney sweep who lives with his wife, Marylou, in Vermont. He spends his time woodworking, fishing, hiking and volunteering to help the families of veterans actively serving in Iraq and Afghanistan.

Resources

- Scriptures taken from the Holy Bible, New International Version®, NIV®. Copyright © 1973, 1978, 1984 by Biblica, Inc.™ Used by permission of Zondervan. All rights reserved worldwide. www.zondervan.com.

- Scriptures taken from the Holy Bible, King James Version, Thomas Nelson, Inc., 1984.

- Mally Cox-Chapman, The Case for Heaven, G.P. Putnam's Sons, 1995.

- The Oxford Companion to the Bible, Oxford University Press, 1993.

- Cover photograph taken July 31, 2010, by Ned Edwards of Edwards Images Photography (www.edwardsimages.com).

- Kelly Lanigan, Vietnam War Battle Series: Sappers Take a Beating at Liberty Bridge, VFW Magazine, March 2008.

Phil Young offers special thanks to journalist Kelly Lanigan for his article, which provided the details of a day that had been missing for almost forty years.

LaVergne, TN USA
12 November 2010
204596LV00005B/1/P